SAY IT LOUD

Rochelle Brock and Richard Greggory Johnson III
Executive Editors

Vol. 32

The Black Studies and Critical Thinking series
is part of the Peter Lang Education list.
Every volume is peer reviewed and meets
the highest quality standards for content and production.

PETER LANG
New York • Washington, D.C./Baltimore • Bern
Frankfurt • Berlin • Brussels • Vienna • Oxford

REGINA A. BERNARD-CARREÑO

SAY IT LOUD

Black Studies, Its Students, and Racialized Collegiate Culture

PETER LANG
New York • Washington, D.C./Baltimore • Bern
Frankfurt • Berlin • Brussels • Vienna • Oxford

Library of Congress Cataloging-in-Publication Data
Bernard-Carreño, Regina.
Say it loud: black studies, its students, and racialized
collegiate culture / Regina A. Bernard-Carreño.
p. cm. — (Black studies and critical thinking; vol. 32)
Includes bibliographical references and index.
1. African Americans—Study and teaching (Higher)
2. African American college students. 3. African Americans—Education (Higher)
4. Education, Higher—Aims and objectives—United States. I. Title.
E184.7.B47   378.1'982996073—dc23   2013012581
ISBN 978-1-4331-1583-7 (hardcover)
ISBN 978-1-4331-1582-0 (paperback)
ISBN 978-1-4539-1035-1 (e-book)
ISSN 1947-5985

Bibliographic information published by **Die Deutsche Nationalbibliothek**.
Die Deutsche Nationalbibliothek lists this publication in the "Deutsche
Nationalbibliografie"; detailed bibliographic data is available
on the Internet at http://dnb.d-nb.de/.

© 2014 Peter Lang Publishing, Inc., New York
29 Broadway, 18th floor, New York, NY 10006
www.peterlang.com

All rights reserved.
Reprint or reproduction, even partially, in all forms such as microfilm,
xerography, microfiche, microcard, and offset strictly prohibited.

Contents

	Acknowledgments	vii
1.	Introduction	1
2.	Lena James and Felicity Porter: The Television Depiction of Black Girl Identity at College	11
3.	Making Black Studies Political	25
4.	The Black Outcast in the Classroom: Street Lit and Black Academics	62
5.	Black Studies Projects: The Communal Class, Samples and Resources	82
6.	Scholarship and Community	97
	Bibliography	107
	Notes	113

Acknowledgments

To my little family, again, another massive thank you for each nudge, reminder, and every example of loving support you have shown me throughout this process. For months and years on end, you have allowed me to freely arrange my teaching schedules and hold "office hours" well into the night and by mobile communication in the wee hours of the morning. You have accepted the constant tapping away on my BlackBerry to respond to the endless emails from students during our meals and "family time" together. You did not mind me trading my time with you all in order to teach a Black Studies class on Saturdays and shoved me into the arms of those who wanted more information. That experience turned out to be truly amazing, and one I could not have guessed would be my own. I am eternally grateful for your belief in my work and your lessons of solidarity, compassion, and humanity. This is for you.

To my mother, Ethel, you are truly an inspiration, always have been. Many people say that to one another ("you are my inspiration"), and while for them it has a sense of truth, for me, it is my reality. I really don't know anything else to believe. There is no better reference in this entire universe. As I continue to "go on and teach the kids about something," I have learned from your strength and hope that even in my weakest moment, I make you proud. It has been my life's goal to do this, and each step I take, I have you at the top. To my sister and brother, you both make my family circle totally complete, and I am so comforted to know that our love and solidarity for one another close the gap in our distance. Again to my husband, what another journey this has been. Just when I thought I couldn't go any further, you reminded me that this has been my life's work all along, and that the future work of the young people depends on projects and examples like these. Thank you for extending yourself, the time it takes to encourage another. Thank you for sharing lessons of blessings even when in dark moments they are entirely undiscoverable.

Another special thank you to Chris Myers and Rochelle Brock for believing in this project, and giving me the room I needed to wade through the politics of academia while trying to write a version of the truth. I am so thankful we are all on the same team. To everyone at Lang who worked on this project, I thank you.

To my students and to the students who participated in many of the workshops: the popularity of my classes and my work would never have become the burning bush it has been had it not been for my early undergraduate students who still believe in the power of critical pedagogy. The "Profo-Clan" was a blessing I'd never trade, no matter what identity is in offer. To my colleagues who became friends and confidants in the struggle, especially Professor Arthur Lewin who read several versions of various chapters and offered me honest critique, and told me when I was perhaps "talking crazy." Through your friendship, I am inspired to continue pursuing the revolutionary work of those before me. Thank you for being there, and reminding me this is the work that needs to be done; everything else is simple and foolish.

Last, but never least, to my beautiful little boy Carter Blu and my darling daughter Sophia Gray. You both came into my life just when the world, our family, and I, needed you the most. You have taught me patience, kindness, compassion, and have given me an insurmountable definition of humanity and peace. When you begin to see the world as it really is, I hope you too will continue to fight to make the world just a little more just and comforting. You are both undefeatable and an incredible source of motivation. I love every inch of you both. This is for you too.

—R.

CHAPTER ONE

Introduction

As I write this introduction, Occupy Wall Street (OWS) has quieted down, but still remains in a position that challenges the socially unjust, now globally, and so are the student movements/protests all over the world. These demonstrations have been met with heavy-handed law enforcement and brutality against young student protestors. These movements are undeniably important, as issues like tuition hikes, poverty, and a breakdown in humanity become more and more pressing. Yet there is an attempt to quiet the brewing storm without considering why it's stirring. To silence them, or ignore them, is to ignore change.

This book started out as a 10-year chronicling project. By 2001, as a pioneer of the graduate program in African American Studies at Columbia University, I had been the first student to complete my Master's degree in African American Studies. I was also immersed in Black Studies as an Assistant Editor of the Malcolm X Project at the Institute for Research in African American Studies (IRAAS), also at Columbia, founded and directed by the late Dr. Manning Marable. My work at the IRAAS allowed me to collaborate with both young and established scholars of Black Studies and made me determined to continue investigating such programs. After completing my editorship and my Master's degree, I began doctoral studies in Urban Education at the Graduate Center, City University of New York. I remember that countless people in academia told me that a graduate degree in African American Studies would only be beneficial if I planned to obtain a doctorate in the field. Some discouraged me from applying to such programs, and others encouraged me to continue thinking about ways in which I could secure my place in such an academic department. The world, they said, "held no legitimate jobs in this field."

> The point is that very few degrees in the arts and social sciences relate directly to a profession, unless it is in teaching, and even this is not cut and dried. (Christian, 2007, 354)

In junior high school I read incessantly and became addicted to the writers of the Harlem Renaissance. Every week I found myself at the Coliseum Bookstore on Broadway in New York City, searching for new authors. My school library was dominated by "famous" White authors who spoke of romantic notions that were forbidden to me. High school seemed to eliminate the voices, writings, and discussions about the Harlem Renaissance altogether. In college I was invited back into the world of Black Studies by my English professor, a young White male who knew the genre as well as his own life experiences. They were part of him and part of who he had become as an educator. I took four classes with him and saw how he found ways to include Black writers at every point in the syllabus—whether the class focused on Black culture or not. He knew the importance of introducing and cultivating a conversation on Black writers, regardless of the overarching course's content. I fell in love with Zora Neale Hurston all over again. She was not just hanging on the shelves of a bookstore's "African American" section—she was present in his college classrooms, and we were critically decoding her messages. This, among many other reasons for intellectual pursuit, led me to write this book.

In 2003, I was hired by a Black and Latino/a Studies department in New York City. Although I had been officially studying the plights of Urban Education and had already completed my first Master's degree in African American Studies, the teaching job at this very small department began to increase my growth in the study and catapulted the chronicling project. At the time of my hire, I was already teaching education courses at a graduate school only a train ride away from my new position. I found myself teaching courses in education that connected urban Black narratives to urban pedagogy in traditional settings (university classrooms). My chair at the time encouraged me to teach courses in both Black and Latino/a Studies and suggested that my "interdisciplinary scholarship" and "numerous trainings" made me unique and valuable to the department. Since I was able to teach both racialized academic sequences, I could offer classes that intertwined multiple racial, social, and theoretical narratives. Although I was just an adjunct, my chair offered me high-demand courses such as "Introduction to African American Studies" and also gave me the opportunity to develop courses based on my own expertise and interests. He encouraged diversity in the course offerings and in many ways reflected the mode of critical inquiry in which I had been trained.

When I first began teaching my block of classes, I realized the students needed an introduction to "Introduction to African American Studies." My students reminded me of my own college classmates: they wanted to be around "Blackness" because their own identities, whether positive and affirmed or curious and struggling, would find comfort there. They found solidarity just being around Black students and Black faculty because "every other group sticks to themselves." Many stated this as the reason they took Black Studies classes. There was comfort in being around dialogue about people of their "own kind." Yet these students were not prepared to look into the historical analyses and presentations of Black Studies. They were not grounded in a scholarly approach to the subject; they had been introduced to the Black narrative at a college level only indirectly, through traditional classes such as English. Their experiences with Black Studies had been the all-too-familiar "Black History Month" lessons in high school, later reproduced by out-of-touch faculty members who excluded them from shaping the discussions. Thus, the students began to exclude the faculty from theirs.

Year after year, students revisited popular civil rights leaders during February teaching units and sometimes read Baldwin in their college freshman English classes (though never gay Baldwin, only Black radical Baldwin). For most of them, their introduction to Black Studies began and ended there. Socio-politically, many believed being Black warranted expert scholarship in the field. The story was repetitive, and Black Studies became a social lair for students, as opposed to an academic hub for production and consumption of knowledge (Bernard-Carreño, 2010). They had no idea that Black Studies still remains a political and social movement. No one had taught them the reason Black Studies exists, except perhaps one professor. However, as you will see in the chapters that follow, this one professor, a 35-year veteran in the field, can only do so much without institutional support and faculty camaraderie. In the end, dedicated professors of Black Studies not only tire of their teaching loads but also lead double lives. They teach professionally (and perhaps it makes them who they are), but they also work to uplift the race (as was the case with Anna Julia Cooper).

When I first began teaching Black Studies courses, I surveyed the students and was stunned to find out that they had never read Manning Marable, Patricia Hill Collins, bell hooks, or Amiri Baraka and had read only passages from Nella Larsen's *Passing*, Zora Neale Hurston's *Their Eyes Were Watching God*, James Baldwin's *The Fire Next Time*, and selections of Richard Wright's writings (particularly *Black Boy*). Many said Wright's books were too complex and too long to comprehend. Outright and quite visible was their rejection of academic Black writing. They complained that the books I assigned were "too hard" and that they were spending more time "with a dictionary" than actually reading and understanding. While not buying into the "too difficult" argument, I knew I had to find ways to get the students talking about what they were reading and create a way for them to compare and connect their overall learning experience with their own intellectual development. I changed the readings and offered a progression of texts from comical to traditionally academic (what I call 'the heavies'). The revised course had a progression of difficulty and thus a built-in sense of literate achievement. After combatting complaints about the books (and the class for that matter) being "too complicated," I assigned *Because You Don't Read the Newspaper* (2000), a graphic novel by Aaron McGruder. The students loved it. Colleagues questioned the legitimacy of assigning a "comic book" for a college course and believed it to be "juvenile." Whatever they thought it was, I still believe the pedagogical move was a good one. The students were able to fully digest, and then critically analyze, the political positions of the "Black struggle" through the perspective of two adolescent cartoon characters (Huey and Riley). They used McGruder's work when reading more complex ideas about Black political ideology—in fact, the comic offered history in a contemporary perspective, held more of their interest, and provided more of a connection to their other texts. It was perhaps one of the six assigned books that they did not resell to the bookstore. They kept it in their personal collection, where "schoolbooks" do not always have permanent residency.

When designing the syllabi for the various courses I was given to teach in Black Studies, I spent hours perusing libraries, bookstores, and online book inventories to find material for my students. Some seasoned professors asked why I would constantly change the reading materials and give myself "more work"— their own notes yellowing with age, their content outdated to the life experiences of their students. I knew the strictly academic titles I had been reading during my research hours would not directly or immediately appeal to all of their interests. Sure, with enough quizzes, formal exams, and research papers, the students could memorize anything to pass a class, but would they get it? Pedagogically, I do not participate in the promotion of rote memorization games or skill development. I began making trips to street vendor tables in Harlem and in the West Village to observe what customers were buying, to take in the conversations customers were having with these street vendors who were clearly organic intellectuals (Bernard-Carreño, 2010). I came across a brand new copy of *The Coldest Winter Ever* (1999) by Sister Souljah. An older Black woman said to me, "That's the best book I ever read." I didn't need any more confirmation. I handed the vendor my seven dollars, and began reading the book on the train ride home. Part of me knew this book, like McGruder's, would send off administrative alarms, but another part of me knew that my students needed a connection. My students were being inundated with traditional academics in their other classes. In my class I had to create "release time," but one that was still of the highest intellectual order, albeit with flexibility in achieving the standard.

Assigning *The Coldest Winter Ever* alongside *Pedagogy of the Oppressed* (Freire, 1970)[1] was one of the best moves I ever made. The students immediately developed a critical lens because of the contrasting yet related books, particularly with *The Coldest Winter Ever*. Some of the students, who were not members of an "at risk" population and had never gotten into the type of trouble depicted in the book, nevertheless completely identified with the protagonist's environmental landscape. The majority of the students in that class, however, knew the "streets" well. Another large portion of the class found school to be the antithesis of the streets, and a major reason why they chose to attend college was to get away from that environment. They dissected Souljah's book in all of its 400 pages with ease, with dialogical finesse, and wrote some of the best papers I have ever read. The students spent a good portion of the time juxtaposing their own narratives to this "street lit" title, while also considering the breadth of their own communities. They found books like Souljah's to be personal, relatable, and current. Encountering these titles in the course gave them the avenue to read the more traditional texts. They needed an introduction to Introduction to African American Studies, and to my surprise, that introduction did not include a basic lesson into the history of the struggle. That seemed to arise naturally out of discussion instead of within a text. They needed to see how their own struggles could be reflected in contemporary writings before they were willing to accept historical struggles as part of their personal narratives. They needed to see themselves reflected in the course, in the dialogue, and in their assignments. They needed to let their voices out from the trappings that traditional intellectual pursuit can cause. They needed to be themselves at least twice a week, for an hour and fifteen minutes at a time.

After *The Coldest Winter Ever*, I taught *Push* (1996) by Sapphire. Years later, I still receive emails about the "*Push* experience in class," particularly after the movie was released in 2009. The point here is that students of Black Studies, especially Black students, need to see their own experiences reflected in the class. They need to be able to develop their narrative before and during the process of learning about the Black experience. This type of pedagogy, which requires much preparatory work by the professor, is a wholesome learning experience for everyone involved. To reflect back on the colleague who asked why I assign new books, work every semester to change the class, and give myself more work, I answer in a way that illustrates that teaching is about growth: in the process of changing the course outline repeatedly, I too grow. A field as rich as Black Studies cannot allow repetition. Many scholars have said that in order for Black Studies to be self-sustaining and supported, the field must grow and continue to produce scholars and scholarship (Christian, 2007).

Since my early days as a Black and Latino/a Studies adjunct, I have continued chronicling the experiences of teaching Black Studies and have come to know the students throughout their 4-plus years of college pursuit. I have listened closely to their anxieties about schooling, their intellectual and professional pursuits, and the juggling of their personal lives. Most of the students I chronicled for this project have minored in Black Studies, because their school offered no major in the field. Many of my own students did not realize that Black Studies was a major at other schools within their university system and while that information is publicly available, there is no fervor behind its promotion. Some students have gone on to create Black Studies majors for themselves through ad hoc major programs. Others have come from other schools within the city, taken classes at night and weekends through university permits, and capitalized on consortium opportunities. The information about race—i.e., Black Studies—is available, the students have a desire for it, but the fight for its popularity has perhaps lost a bit of its blaze.

The movements and experiences that led me to write this book are not the same experiences I had near the completion of the book. When I began chronicling the experiences of teaching and the narrative experiences of Black Studies students, there was a fire among them. Something political and not restful was brewing among them. They wanted change but didn't know what it would do for them and had no clear agenda or plan for executing it. Yet, they knew they were not afraid to pursue the change they were in search of. They weren't hesitant to spend hours with me in my cramped "part-timer" office to discuss the world, their plights, and the plight of Black Studies. They weren't afraid to fight, and time seemed to stand still when we were together. As you will see throughout the chapters, this fighting pulse among the Black Studies students was incredibly strong early on in my time with them, but throughout the years, many of them (my own students and those who contributed their sentiments to my project) have been streamlined by the requirements of their majors and their professional endeavors. This strain and individualistic training created a backseat position for their fight for Black Studies. Having lost a sense of urgency for Black Studies to be offered as a major at their particular school, many of the students, while less than satisfied, kept a strong relationship with the faculty members who became mentors to them. However, they did not pursue change in the field of Black Studies. They were enticed by the applause and recognition they received as they pursued individual achievements and change in other areas. Black Studies was no longer at the frontline of their fighting urge. They seemed happy to be able to earn a Black Studies minor with only three courses, allowing them to pay more attention to their major degree of study.

> […] Even students with a keen interest in Black studies tend to double major with another, more traditional discipline (Christian, 2007, 354).

Students were also happy to maintain relationships with selected Black Studies faculty members, with whom they could engage in dialogue and approach for advice and letters of recommendation. Yet, none seemed interested in pursuing Black Studies at graduate school, unless they were already majoring in the field. A minor simply was not enough to pique long-term interest.

Throughout this book, you will be introduced to some of the media representations that shape Black students' perceptions of "college life" and how they use these models to pursue their own experiences in college. This is particularly true for female Black students. Along this strand of media representations of Black "college life," you will also read what happens when these television examples do not follow through into realities. The disconnect between presentation and reality then urges students to begin pursuing other areas of study, while still looking to establish connectivity to Black identity among friends on campus and Black narratives in their classes. To produce a thorough analysis of the scope and severity of Black Studies experiences, I often held both formal and informal forums on Black Studies and Black identity on and off campus. These group settings, which sometimes took the form of Black Studies workshops, led to some of the most valuable information for any educator in any field, particularly in preparing a book like this. These workshops and open forums allowed me to ask brazen questions and to receive open and honest (and sometimes brutal) answers.

I felt it was important to present those ideas and sentiments in this book if Black Studies academics are to begin considering more carefully the population that they teach. The goal of this book is to give space to the traditional academic experience but still be truthful to the experiences of Black Studies and its students. It is folly to think that their off-campus lives do not affect, inspire, and alter the ways in which they try to obtain college degrees. It is also a blunder to think that schools offer all they can to shape well-rounded student identities. Many schools tend to assume that Black Studies students are all Black. While among majors that may be largely true, other racial groups do register for Black Studies classes and major and minors in the field. The responses of non-Black students to questions about Black Studies, whether they took the class as an "ethnic studies" requirement or elective, are crucial to overall perceptions about the field. In this book, I have included their voices wherever possible, in order to give the reader examples of how tied to the history of struggle these students also are. They may perhaps have different motivations, but they too are inspired.

While many of the chapters critique Black Studies narratives and programs, readers should keep in mind the complexity of the program offerings, the politics surrounding the schools and administrations and the students' identities, all in an effort to make these programs inclusive of all the students who wish to study the field. It is also important to remember that this book chronicles the experiences at just two schools and thus focuses on the complexities of small programs as opposed to large and well-recognized Black Studies departments. I felt it important to discuss small Black Studies programs, as they are the most at risk of department closures, the administrative threat of such, and internal turmoil as they struggle with finances, faculty turnover, low registrations, class closures, racism, sexism, ageism, and uneven student interest.

In the second chapter of *Say It Loud*, I discuss the impact of television programming that depicts collegiate culture and life, both Black and White. Black students are not just watching shows about Black college experiences (and these shows are extremely limited), but they are also watching shows about White collegiate culture. This is particularly true for young women of color, who envision their college experience as identical to the television versions—until they show up for class. Although I address media representation of young women of color extensively in my first book *Black and Brown Waves: The Cultural Politics of Young Women of Color and Feminism*, (2009),[2] it was necessary to reintroduce this topic as it relates specifically to the Black college female depicted (or not) on television. With reality television and its stars imposing on the personal lives and aspirations of young women, reintroducing this topic repeatedly reminds an educator that our classrooms are not the only influence we need to consider. We have to continue to seek out creative ways to combat negative stereotypes and messages in order to get and keep these students excited about learning. This is particularly important when Black Studies is only offered as a minor; in such cases, students may forget the topic all together if there is no personal connection.

The depiction of Black college life on television is limited and typically presents either the "Black token" at the predominantly White school (they are usually voiceless or somewhere in the background), or the Black student at the all-Black school (usually female, loud, and sassy). Neither of these offerings remotely prepares Black Studies students for the commuter-collegiate culture experience—where Black Studies may not be a major, where Black fraternity and sorority chapters may not exist, and where the Black Student Union may be represented as a "party club" without any intellectual substance. Although many schools use and throw around the term "diversity" (sometimes for extended university funding and magazine spreads), it is usually based on student enrollment, not retention. Faculty are not always included in the "diversity" dialogue either. As one student suggested during an open forum

> […] there's no diversity here except when it comes to the immigrant students or the international students. That's what the school is using to claim that it's 'diverse.' (Shauna, Black, Senior)

My analysis of two major shows depicting collegiate culture (one for Whites and one for Blacks) is an introduction to the college scenarios Black students imagine before they arrive on campus—either they are not the majority, or Black Studies is sought after not for academics, but for collegiate relationships.

In subsequent chapters, I consider the role of the Black Studies educator. To analyze only students is to miss an important piece of the Black Studies puzzle. To fill this gap, I introduce a discussion on the Black Studies pedagogy and the faculty role in the production of such an academic field. Students that participated in many of the forums were candid about their feelings towards non-Black professors teaching courses in Black Studies and were also candid about their expectations for Black Studies professors and the content of such courses. Most of these responses and attitudes were included in this book to give the reader a clear depiction of student-centered emotional attachments and disengagements from the topic and the faculty who were bound to the various departments for a variety of reasons.

Building on those discussions, I also include an analysis of the historical underpinnings of Black Studies programs. I not only critique such programs that do not respond to student interest or demand, but I also offer resources and remedies for department and program building. These chapters present a version of the history and a current analysis as to how Black Studies has to remain political, just as it had been in its incubation stage. Historically and in our present day, the political fight for Black Studies has always been in the interest of students, particularly Black students and students within other marginalized groups. In addition, it has always been a student-led movement fought with intellectual stamina and passionate tenacity. In chapter 4, I provide a detailed analysis of what Black Studies looked like early in its 1960s infancy and how, to some degree, it has remained political—tied with student activism and community building. Here, I also include student responses on what Black Studies stands for today and what it should represent in the future. Considering the socio-political positioning of Black Studies on college campuses, whether a minor or a major degree of study, I also write about how the inclusion of unconventional material (such as street lit) is important to the overall presentation of Black Studies—to Black students in particular but also to other students who may take the course. The inclusion of organic ideologies and writings such as street lit gives students perspective on producing and consuming knowledge that has not been presented to them in popular or competitive ways. This lends itself to the production of innovative and competitive ways of learning.

In considering Black Studies programs, faculty, and variations of information, I also include an analysis on the continuum of Black Studies, using what I call the "Black Bookstore as Think-Tank" model. This model was developed when I began to consider how students who had only pursued a minor in Black Studies could continue to learn more. Developing relationships with many independent bookstores in New York City (where I order course books), I expose students to non-traditional environments where they can seek new information and new ways of finding it. I want to give them a Coliseum Bookstore moment that I've so often had—first as a child, then again as a teen, hungry for information overload. During this project, I discovered (among many other things) that historically, Black bookstores were used as study hubs and political infusers. With the diminishment of such culturally stimulating and cultural think tanks as Black bookstores, Black Studies minors are deprived of places where they can examine topics more closely while also making strong ties to Black communities. Ultimately, these bookstores are failing to meet student needs and fall short in presenting a clear picture of a field with such historical and contemporary critical inquiry. Without these types of think tanks, academic programs that are already limited and struggling, are less likely to house an abundance of curious minds and are less likely to develop a student base with the experience to demand better programmatic material.

While writing this book has been a journey of chronicling achievements and failures of Black Studies programs, as well as the experiences of both teaching and learning Black Studies, it only just begins to truly unpack the subject. *Say It Loud* is an examination of existing programs and ideological practices, alongside Black student narratives, but can just as easily be used to produce a new set of ideas in the field of Black Studies. If we are legitimate and competitive in preparing our Black Studies students, whether as their major degree of study or in their minor pursuit, we create a generation of thinkers who can also work—not merely one or the other.

CHAPTER TWO

Lena James and Felicity Porter

The Television Depiction of Black Girl Identity at College

What does a college girl on television usually look like? As much as we would like to rack our brains and begin putting her together in our minds, the media will prove she is almost universally the same. She appears on television shows as young, White, blond, and is far less than intellectually competitive. Whether she is a White buxom beauty in a slapstick comedy like *Accepted* (2006) starring Blake Lively or a nerd transformed into another White buxom beauty like Carla Gugino in *Son in Law* (1993), her intelligence has no place on the screen. Hollywood movies and television shows alike have set clear stereotypes and an even clearer model for what girls should look like as college students. Early films depicting collegiate culture featured male characters in central roles. Films like *Animal House* (1978), *Revenge of the Nerds* (1984), *Back to School* (1985), *With Honors* (1994), *Good Will Hunting* (1997), *How High* (2001), *Slackers* (2002), and *College* (2008) have showcased the humorous and seriousness of the college "White boy." Collegiate culture for women (on television) has been the presentation of the White female, who is overly sexualized and appears in the backdrop of the White male pursuit of knowledge. For many girls, particularly on screen (and particularly White), they experience what I call *identity-trading*. Identity-trading takes the form of trading current self-images for complete makeovers or creating fictional selves to improve social standings and interactions as they navigate the dual worlds of school and real life.

This chapter will present a close examination and analysis of various television shows and their complexities, discussing the intersections of race, class, and gender as related to the production of the college girl of color on television. For many viewers, these television shows are first examples of collegiate culture, and thus identity-trading is inevitable. Many films and television shows alike have made a mockery out of the collegiate experience for women of color, who are either in the background of a non-important scene or invisible altogether. White girls are presented through an upper middle class lens; they share a desire to obtain a higher social standing, which ultimately includes some form of over-sexualization and objectification. To obtain these goals, characters are created and scripted into joining sororities, engaging in sometimes illegal behavior or activities, and most importantly, stripping themselves of all intellectual capabilities unless it may assist in wooing a potential suitor. Women of color have very different roles and their presentation on television is even less flattering.

In 1999, actresses Mo'Nique and Countess Vaughn starred in the television sitcom *The Parkers*, which depicts an African American mother–daughter team who decide to attend Santa Monica Community College together. Mo'Nique plays the mother (Nikki) who gave birth to her daughter Kim (Vaughn) when she was 15 years old. Nikki was forced to drop out of high school, so pursuing college alongside her daughter means several things for the characters and several other things for the audience. For five seasons, the show followed Nikki's romantic pursuit of "Professor Oglevee" (Dorien Wilson). Celebrity cameos and R&B performances appeared in various episodes. For the Parker women, college always seemed to be stressful and a complete nuisance compared to all their other social aspirations and/or activities. *The Parkers* ran from 1999–2004. The show's finale drew in 3.6 million viewers[1] anxiously awaiting Nikki's decision to marry Prof. Oglevee.[2] The same amount of anxiety never mounted over whether either of the two women would graduate from college.

During about the same time frame as *The Parkers*, the WB Television Network released *Felicity*, which presented the opposite narrative of *The Parkers*. *Felicity* debuted in 1998 with a 7.1 million viewership.[3] The plot was quite simple. Although the character "Felicity" is accepted to a Pre-Med program at Stanford University, she chooses to attend college in New York City to follow her high school crush—simply because at her high school graduation, he writes in her yearbook that he wished he had gotten to know her.

The contrast between the two shows provides the opportunity to critically analyze a depiction of collegiate culture based on racial presentation. *The Parkers* is framed in the comfort of a sitcom. The humor allows the guilty pleasure of laughing along with two heavy-set Black women who are attending college (at least for 30 minutes a day). Felicity, on the other hand, a young White female who falls victim to infatuation and chooses her "dream man" instead of her "dream career," provides viewers with emotion, some drama, and a certain academic presence, even in misguided form. The Black female college student is comical and sassy. The White female college student, if not a sex object, is presented in what some would consider a post-feminist state of mind. Both depictions are less than positive. Although interpretively the various images of college girls on television all have a different narrative, in every case her goal is the same. She serves to entertain, not necessarily to inspire. Even less prominent is her goal to consume and/or produce knowledge. Her learning, or what she is able to express through her character, has less to do with her own academic aspirations than it has to do with her social mobility in school. In short, she is not advertising the pursuit of an education for intellectual purposes.

The humor of *The Parkers* stems from Nikki's inability to successfully fit into a college environment, as would a "young" and "traditional" student. To combat this awkwardness, Nikki clings to her teenage daughter in her attempts at social navigation and mobility.[4] Like many past and present stereotypes of Black characters on television, *The Parkers* are loud women: overweight, sassy, and focused on everything but their education goals.

Another contrast to *The Parkers* is Bill Cosby's *A Different World*, which aired for six years (1987–1993). For many young women of color, this show created a partially positive depiction of young women of color in college. *A Different World* gave viewers a dark-skinned nerd (or two), a light-skinned Southern belle, a loud and sassy girl from the projects, and an "earthy crunchy" environmentalist biracial girl. However, the show was not without fault although with much good intention. Much time was spent depicting not just Black life on campus but Black sorority and fraternity life, and for many students, this is not a reality. Many of these stereotypical depictions of Black college life possibly created a further divide within the racial group. On the show, many of the darker-skinned Black female students were depicted as being extremely "pro-Black": wearing African garb on campus and making references to returning to the "motherland." These same darker-skinned characters went on to pursue their college education with aggression. On the other hand, many of the lighter-skinned characters were portrayed as "earthy crunchy" à la Erykah Badu, or complete "dimwits" such as in the case of the character Whitley Gilbert played by Jasmine Guy and, at times Winifred "Freddie" Brooks played by Cree Summer. At the end of the first season (1988), the only White female character (played by Marisa Tomei) attending "Hillman College" was replaced by Black characters so that "the university" on television appeared more realistic of a Black college to an at-home audience.[5] Aside from Black Greek life, *A Different World* was consistent in trying to become an agent of social change.

While *A Different World* was a 30-minute sitcom and *Felicity* a one-hour drama, the former was the only example of a program on network television that showcased a predominantly of-color (Black in particular) cast attending college. Currently, there are no one-hour dramas, 30-minute sitcoms, or other programs that depict a predominantly of-color population in a college setting. There is, however, *College Hill* (2004–2009), which was a cable-television reality show based on the lives of students that attend a Historically Black College/University (HSBC).

College Hill shares a great similarity to MTV's *The Real World* and conceivably the name *College Hill* is given to indicate that all housemates are college students, for otherwise there is no direct focus on collegiate work on the show. *College Hill* was at the center of a major controversy in 2007, when the show included students from the University of the Virgin Islands who were engaged in sexually explicit and negative portrayals of Blacks in college. Clearly what the girls were engaged in was identity-trading, only this was through reality television, and not a one-hour drama such as *Felicity*. Yet, Felicity identity-trades as well. However, hers appears to be romantic and reflective, not detrimental, as was the case with the University of the Virgin Islands female students.

In *Felicity*'s first episode, the audience is privy to her "hidden" thoughts, as her inner monologue explains why she is sitting in her dorm in New York City instead of at a Pre-Med program at Stanford. She is recounting through tape recorder to a friend (they tape letters instead of writing them) her decision to be in New York for college. The story is as follows: Felicity's high school crush signed her yearbook, indicating how much he admired her and how much time he spent thinking about who she was but never took the time to get to know exactly *who* she was. In a hurried decision, throwing caution to the wind (in a stereotypically ultra-feminine way), Felicity takes flight to the big city, with no friends awaiting her arrival, except the crush who has no idea she is also headed to New York. Felicity is bright-eyed and clearly excited about being in New York, but none of these characteristics or desires points directly to her education at the "University of New York." Mid-season, Felicity is even more focused on her love interest, as she is caught in a love triangle with the high school crush, Ben Covington (played by Scott Speedman), and her college resident advisor Noel Crane (played by Scott Foley).

While Felicity herself serves as an unofficial tutor to both men, her intellectual abilities are highlighted through helping them "read" and "understand" poetry (the "soft" and "emotional" subject). We can thus begin to perhaps consider Felicity as being clearly skilled, at least in the Humanities. In 1996, a study conducted by Dr. Nancy Signorelli, Children Now (California) and the Kaiser Foundation found that 34 percent of women on television were shown "using their intelligence," and 35 percent exposed and stressed "self reliance" on television and in movies.[6] It is imperative that Felicity be "dumbed-down" in order for her character and her show to survive. Superficially she seems "smart" or at least "studious," but her intelligence is used in tricky ways, and her self-reliance can be translated as a youthful resistance towards her parents. In many ways, this is an attempt to cryptically and stereotypically "feminize" the character by constructing her as a science major but creating a softer side of her by depicting poetry and the humanities as a private passion. Some readers may even see Felicity's private pedagogy not as an exposure of her intelligence but as a silent hope of establishing a romantic relationship in exchange for lessons about poetry. This is Felicity's participation in identity-trade.

In *Gender on Campus: Issues for College Women* (1998), Sharon Bohn Gmelch writes that although in the late 1980s, women were appearing on television more than before, they were being portrayed in stereotypical contexts. Gmelch considers the following three contexts: (1) romantic interests, (2) home, and (3) family.[7] Felicity herself falls very neatly into all of these categories. She is primarily interested in pursuing a love relationship with her former high school crush. She is undoubtedly facing self-management at 17, as she is liberated from parental control, and—apparently for the first time—is rebelling against their wishes. Her active participation in the identity-trade as a private pedagogue for two potential lovers easily defines her task at self-management. Last, Felicity is creating a new family structure for herself by way of her circle of college friends. She is not independent of the media's making her a product of White privilege, not particularly pro-feminist, or feminist herself. She certainly cannot survive without two men being interested in her. After all, pursuing a man was her sole motivation for attending the University of New York. Her intellectual epiphany that suggests the importance of her academic career (whether in humanities or science) does not arrive until 2001, nearly the end of the show's run.

Another dimension of the show is what the University of New York is able to offer Felicity aside from parent-free self-reliance and management. Although the larger argument here about Felicity is that her importance and intelligence rely on the unfolding of two love interests (her poetic tutelage), the racial juxtaposition to other shows is important here as well. College, to Felicity, offers academic freedom. Her being White, young, and economically stable facilitates the freedom she experiences at the University of New York. The importance of considering race and social class an adhesive to gender is also to consider the way one begins to understand how the opposite of Felicity is presented. For example, Felicity, although given a "dream" opportunity to attend Stanford for Pre-Med, makes her own choice(s). When told that the choice she has made will leave her financially unsupported by both her parents, she takes a work-study job. Now, a student applying for work-study must be from a specifically-proven low socioeconomic background which neither Felicity nor her parents are members of. The United States Department of Education's website clearly states the preliminary factors when considering work-study cases. They are as follows:

> The fundamental elements in this standard formula are the student's income (and assets, if the student is independent), the parents' income and

assets (if the student is dependent), the family's household size, and the number of family members (excluding parents) attending postsecondary institutions. The EFC is the sum of: (1) a percentage of net income (remaining income after subtracting allowances for basic living expenses) and (2) a percentage of net assets (assets remaining after subtracting an asset protection allowance).[8]

Felicity's eligibility for this type of employment is questionable in the real world, particularly since her father is able to make a simple phone call and have her re-admitted to Stanford after denying an original offer of acceptance. Additionally, the University of New York offers Felicity the opportunity to fluctuate between her interests between science and the humanities because she is not confined by a scholarship or other type of aid that requires the maintenance of an acceptable G.P.A. in a particular program. During what seems to be the first week of school, Felicity is already able to attend a party and hit a local college hangout to share a couple of drinks with friends. In short, all of these details show that Felicity has *access*. In a small time span, she can access a government and/or federally funded job on campus, she has access to a social network and scene complete with a couple of love interests, and she has full access to academic opportunities and avenues. Of the nine major characters on the show, including Felicity, four are female. Of the four females, one is of color (Black) and three are White.

The Black female character, Elena Tyler (played by Tangi Miller) is depicted as far more driven than Felicity. Elena is an actual Pre-Med student who hails from a widowed-father household. Although she is depicted positively—confident and more academically driven than Felicity—Miller's character only appears in 65 of the 84 total episodes. Furthermore, Elena comes from an impoverished neighborhood, and college is a way for her to "make something of herself." Felicity in fact is the one to locate the scholarship that allows Elena to continue her academic career. In response to this gesture, Elena becomes immediately and immensely angry with Felicity, suspended in embarrassment as her impoverished background is discovered. Yet, this does not prevent Elena from having an affair with one of her professors, dating a virgin, and leaving a man at the altar.[9] Elena has a chaotic life as she tries to pursue her degree. Felicity, although in a love triangle and undecided about an academic focus, appears less disorganized than her Black roommate.

College Girl of Color

Television shows, especially one-hour dramas, are addictive if relatable to the viewer's life. Ontological relationships to these shows help the viewer decide who they will become, who they despise, how much they relate to and how much of themselves will be invested in the people they watch on television.

For Lena James (played by Jada Pinkett) of the hit series *A Different World*, college bears little resemblance to Felicity's experience. Lena first appeared on the show in 1991 as a freshman who has been classified as an Engineering major but later trades that for a major in Journalism. Like Elena Tyler, she is interested in science, but something prevents her from pursuing the field with total focus. She is from a rough Baltimore housing project. She rolls her eyes at most people, snaps and slides her neck like a snake when she speaks, is very quick at the mouth and is incredibly if not obnoxiously sassy. She has mentioned several times over the seasons that she is in school to avoid "being on the corner, doin' nothing,' and endin' up with a baby."[10] Like Felicity, she appears to have a work-study job, but Lena cleans tables at the campus eatery—clearly not a job that promotes competitive-industry skill building like Felicity's part time work at the admissions office. On her second appearance on *A Different World*, we learn (as does the entire classroom in this scene) that Lena is a graduate of Lincoln High School in Baltimore and is on a partial Engineering scholarship while at the bottom of the curve in her Math class. Also on her academic file is her own accusation that *Romeo and Juliet* is a "foreign language" and was perhaps "written for a cookbook entry." She "can't get with it," as she indicates to her English professor. After failing one of her Math exams, she rouses her classmates to rip up their failed examinations and throw them at the teacher, leaving him standing alone in the room without a class to profess to. The teacher (played by Kadeem Hardison) launches into a diatribe of a monologue about his own father, a bus driver in Brooklyn, who did not have a chance to attend college. He declares that every student in the classroom has an opportunity his father had missed.[11] Everyone in the room, including the teacher, is Black. Hardison goes on to say, "but regardless of your degree, they will think you know less than you do, because you're Black. It's not enough for you to be equal. You have to be better, *we* have to be better, and it's my job to see that *you* and *we* are. I guess I get a little too pumped, but I take this very seriously. So that's where I'm coming from."[12] Lena seems to accept the "tough love" speech and remains in her seat, prepared to learn about Math. Felicity never has an experience like this during her four years at the University of New York. No student at UNY needs an explanation as to why they are there, or what is expected of them; by application to such a school, they already know the reasons. In fact, by season two, although perfectly capable in the sciences, Felicity decides to trade medicine for art, and declares herself a Fine Arts major while holding a secret aspiration for medicine.

In a single episode, during her last season on the show, Lena James is confronted with a duality of her existence, one that is heavily immersed in race and class as an adhesive to gender. In the episode entitled "Homey Don't Ya Know Me" (1993),

Lena and her boyfriend are at a school dance where her ex–best friend and her ex-boyfriend Piccolo (played by Tupac Shakur) show up. Both the exes are from her old Baltimore neighborhood and are complete opposites of her current collegiate crowd. Lena's female best friend is brazen and "street-smart," while Piccolo immediately becomes sexually aggressive towards Lena. By this interaction, we can assume Piccolo has been this aggressive with her in the past: Lena herself is not taken aback. We are asked not to be surprised either, only to await sassy Lena's response. On the other hand, Felicity is 17 and seems sexually innocent upon arrival at college. Lena is not so innocent. This is confirmed when Piccolo states, "I know he [Lena's current college boyfriend] ain't hittin' it like I was, if the boy hittin' it at all."[13] Lena's ex–best friend reinforces the same idea during a private moment of "girl talk" in Lena's dorm room. "Dorien is fine but uh I know he ain't hittin' it like Piccolo was." Lena's only response is "that's none of your business—"[14] a weak defense from someone like Lena James. In the same episode, Lena is also forced to choose between two guys (similar to Felicity), and while both men are of color, in Lena's case, they are socially and economically opposites: as they are defined by character, as "Quiet Boy" (Lena's college boyfriend), and "Joe Hood" (Tupac's character). Therefore, for Lena, college is offering a different set of opportunities. She is not able to use college as the social and intellectual vehicle that gives someone like Felicity an opportunity to (re)invent herself. Instead, she must use college as the escape device, one that will ultimately transport her from danger, poverty, low expectations, and even lower results in pursuit of a "better life." Lena seems more like Elena Tyler. They are almost cut from the same cloth: there are slight changes here and there to recreate a "new" character, but both are based on racial and/or racist stereotypes, rather than original qualities.

Considered here is not simply how the media portray Black female college students but also how these characters become symbols for viewers. Mentioned earlier in this chapter, and here again, is the point that the portrayals of Black collegiate culture on television, for many young girls of color, are first examples of "college life." Many of the students that participated in workshops with me during my years as an adjunct and later as an assistant professor, and again for this project, repeatedly stated that shows about college shaped their reasons for wanting to go to school. They thought "college was really like that." Epistemologically, what makes up the learning environment on television as it is presented to girls? The short answer is that there simply isn't any depiction of what the University of Chicago's Committee on Educational Television (UCCET) has identified as the three traditional objectives of the university (1953)[15]: (1) the acquisition of knowledge, (2) the preservation of knowledge, and (3) the transmission of knowledge. In fact, much of what we see is a failed approach to present positive learning experiences and/or the acquisition, preservation and/or transmission of such knowledge(s) in any of these shows. A year after Lena James arrives on campus, amidst all of her negative and "street culture" characteristics, her character goes further and writes a fallacious essay that wins her a journalism scholarship. A reminder should serve here that Lena was accepted on an Engineering scholarship and thus is also stripped of her scientific abilities in pursuit of the humanities on screen. In *Slate*, David Plotz writes,

> [t]he college drama is problematic because there's little drama, [...] But the drama of the higher-ed experience is internal: What is thrilling about college is the transformation of a chaotic naïve teen-ager into a less chaotic and naïve adult. College students spend their four years in a battle with themselves. Internal debate is not great television.[16]

School of Glam

These shows are conceivably ancient to the college girl of today, yet they are relevant and applicable in many ways. Although *A Different World* ended in the early 1990s, and *Felicity* ended after four (untraditional) years in 2001 (when the tragedy of 9/11 went unaddressed on the show), none of the newer shows has placed Black women in better lights or positive narratives. While some regard *A Different World*, one of the most incredible examples of Black life and culture, as positive (something that could not be found elsewhere on television at the time, or currently), the show did have many faults. Most obvious is that Black Studies was never focused on as a specific course or major of study. Rather, Black Studies is assumed to be part of the whole learning experience because the school is a "Black school" with predominantly "Black students."

In 1988, Lisa Bonet, who played Denise Huxtable on both the *Cosby Show* and on *Different World*, was written out of the show because of her real-life pregnancy. The producers of the show did not feel that the general audience would accept an unwed mother, so her "flakey" character became even more unbalanced as she left college (*A Different World*) to return home, then leave again with her military husband (on the show) to travel Africa alongside his biological daughter. All of this character frazzling was created in order to avoid viewers seeing Denise pregnant and unwed.[17] For many college girls, both the "traditional" and "non-traditional," this pregnancy or motherhood while at school is more of a reality than being able to drop out of school to travel the world. While *A Different World* was a major force in representing Black collegiate culture, in particular Black women, the point remains that there was nothing to compare the show to, except White versions of college girls. Additional changes to *A Different World* also came in the form of writing out the two

White characters altogether. Clearly, this is not what student bodies really look like, and thus represents this idea of racial comfort among every class and within the campus halls; a stark contrast to even the scene at a public university or community college in a place like New York City.

Many of the shows still confirm Plotz's argument that the academic aspect of collegiate culture on television (especially for girls, both Black and other), is still without drama, and leaves viewers unfulfilled and expectant. A more recent depiction of collegiate culture for girls is *Gossip Girl*, the popular teen novel series turned one-hour prime-time teen (and perhaps older) drama. The Wrap website has indicated that *Gossip Girl*'s viewer(s) is an average of 27 years old, and a full 84 percent of viewers are 18 years and older.[18] Yet *Gossip Girl* (both the novels and the television show) is a teen narrative, featuring predominantly White Upper East Side characters, with one or two Black female wallflowers. *Gossip Girl*'s first two seasons are important to the understanding of college girls and race on television. Season two, which aired September 2008–May 2009, focused on all the major characters' preparation for Yale admissions, with one exception of a stray application to Dartmouth College.

The star of *Gossip Girl*, Serena van der Woodsen (played by Blake Lively), is not necessarily stressed over the process of attending college altogether, as she is a celebrity among wealthy socialite New York families. The offer she receives to attend Yale is verbal and results from her socioeconomic status. Her brunette best friend, Blair Waldorf (played by Leighton Meester), who some would consider the star of the show as well, also applies to Yale but simply "isn't good enough" (on paper), although she is equally popular and wealthy. A backdrop character who lives like a "boho," and who producers seem to want to portray as race-less, is Vanessa Abrams, played by biracial actress Jessica Szohr. Vanessa has completed her applications for homeschooling as opposed to an Ivy League college, lives away from her parents, and rooms with her best friend and ex-boyfriend and his family. In addition, as Vanessa neither comes from money nor has any she appears to have an absolute distaste for the wealthy and socially accessed people in her best friend's environment (who attends private school). Although Vanessa is clearly of color, her race is never up for discussion, nor is there any hint that she may not be solely White. In the end however, Vanessa trades in her "hippie" style for a look resembling her Upper East Side friends, complete with an entrance into New York University and a wealthy boyfriend. She too has been created as an identity-trader.

Gossip Girl is much more successful than both *Felicity* and *A Different World*. *Gossip Girl* has extreme drama that does not deal with academics but rather with couture fashion, real fashion designers, and an abundance of sex and scandal, set against a romanticized version of New York schooling which, to a real-life New York undergraduate, seems a farce. Black folks hardly exist on the early seasons of *Gossip Girl* and thus leave the likes of Elena Tyler and Lena James stranded in their stereotypical upbringings. The girls who love such characters do not see themselves represented beyond occasional episodes and short tenures on these shows. They, like their beloved television characters, cannot equate academic growth and intellectual adventures, because it is not valued or represented.

In 1996, the Children Now and the Kaiser Foundation held the 4th Annual Children & Media Conference and produced the *Reflections of Girls in the Media* report. Although their study consisted of all teenage girl respondents, the findings are particularly important and relative to the application of how college women are portrayed on television. The study affirmed that media serve as "powerful teachers."

> For youngsters of all ages, media offer role models, set standards for respect and recognition, define gender, and provide lessons in behavior and appearance.[19]

The irony here is that Black college girls on television have no "powerful teachers," particularly in television-based collegiate settings, unless such teachers are taken from various television personalities and pieced together in an iconic mosaic. Popular organizations like Parental Television Control (PTC) and many feminist-oriented blogs have criticized various shows for their misappropriation and erroneous and/or offensive representation of women, but with no particular attention to Black women or other women of color. The popular blog *Jezebel: Celebrity, Sex, Fashion for Women* ran a topic and online dialogue in June of 2009 entitled, "20 Feminist TV Characters."[20] Notable selected characters included Mary Richards of the *Mary Tyler Moore Show* (1970–1977), Maude Findlay of *Maude* (1972–1978), Marcy D'arcy of *Married with Children* (1987–1997), Julia Sugarbaker and Mary Jo Shively of *Designing Women* (1986–1993), Murphy Brown of *Murphy Brown* (1988–1998), Liz Lemon of *30 Rock* (2006–2013), Elyse Keaton of *Family Ties* (1982–1989), Lisa Simpson of *The Simpsons* (1989–present), Andrea Zuckerman of *Beverly Hills, 90210* (1990–1995), Roseanne Connor of *Roseanne* (1988–1997), Karen Arnold of *The Wonder Years* (1988–1993), Midge Pinciotti of *That '70s Show* (1998–2006), Rory Gilmore of *The Gilmore Girls* (2000–2007), Femme Fatale of *The Powerpuff Girls* (1998–2005), Janice Soprano Baccalieri of the *Sopranos* (1999–2007), Olivia Benson of *Law & Order: SVU*, Miranda Hobbs of *Sex and the City* (1998–2004), and Velma Dinkley of *Scooby-Doo The Venture Bros.* (1969–present). The above list represents women of diverse ages and human capabilities. However, the list is racially exclusive. Of the 20 listed, 11 have either a college degree, a graduate degree, or an assumed stint of and/or completion of university level training. None of the 20 is of color.

The television stereotype is familiar: college girls, and collegiate culture for girls, are mostly White and oversexualized. If she is partially interested in "becoming a doctor," the dream will be replaced by her "feminine emotions" that do not allow her to continue pursuing "real science." At the center of her collegiate journey, there will always be a love interest that she is connected to in more than one way. She will be the love interest and/or she will have a love interest that will distract her from her academic studies: Felicity and Lena had one, and Denise was written off for the inability of the show to give her a boyfriend during her time at school. If she is of color, she will be funny and sassy, the product of an impoverished "ghetto" in some of the most dangerous cities in America, and more than likely be on a partial and/or full scholarship, which causes her incessant worry. She, like her White counterpart, may not continue on the "real science" path, although this may be due to life's social circumstances (losing her scholarship or dropping out) rather than "female emotions." As, in the case of *A Different World* and *Felicity*, each of the two racialized college girls may realize that because she is Black, she may already be at a place of failure. Without recognizing that college is an opportunity that many other people of color do not have access to, she may lose the privilege to do so. On the other hand, a college education presents itself also as an opportunity but not to "get a job" or to escape poverty. Rather, it will present itself as the chance for self-reinvention, complete with heterosexual benefits only accessible away from home, and in a big city. For both women however, sex will always be an important question: perhaps not the seriousness of sexual education but how much sex within the four years a girl can have—unless she is Lena James, who has had sex long before she got to college. Additionally, the Center for the Study of Women in Television and Film at San Diego State University, reported that sexual scenes on television shows have doubled since 1998.

> The study found that 70% of all shows include some sexual content, and that these shows average 5.0 sexual scenes per hour, compared to 56% and 3.2 scenes per hour respectively in 1998, and 64% and 4.4 scenes per hour in 2002. These increases combined represent nearly twice as many scenes of sexual content on TV since 1998.[21]

Young women of color will continue searching for an accurate or closely related depiction of their experiences at college. While no show will ever depict an absolute experience of college culture for girls of color, there is also no show accurately representing any form of relative experiences either.

Misrepresentation on television of Black female college students will perhaps be forever in practice, if such characters are visible at all. Combat strategies presented by many organizations do not seem to be enough to effect the kind of mass change that needs to take place in order to safeguard many young college women from entering competition with television personalities. That said, the organizations have to also begin to take up racial identity-trading cases as well, rather than streamlining the oppression of young women on television as a single example. Reality, and not reality shows, is central to this combat strategy. What many young college women of color need to begin learning how to do is not completely turn the television off and reject at an instant the images they see. This does not always work, as each channel may offer yet another appetizing version. College women of color need to learn the skill of critically examining the characters, shows, and messages that they are watching."[22]

> For women to be seen as being serious about the work of the academy, they must receive (as opposed to claim) a form of schooling the contents of which prepares them to survive and prosper in a world organized by and for men, not women.[23]

What can be discovered if viewed with a critical lens is a typical pattern formation of gender, race, and production/consumption of knowledge (Bernard-Carreño, 2010) on a television campus. The girl on campus, whether she is White or of color, looks the same, has much of the same qualities (just displayed differently), but she is less likely to be a heroine at the end of the show's run. There is much she is in competition with, and this ultimately prevents her from accessing her full academic potential. Organizations like the Center for Screen-Time Awareness[24] and educators alike may encourage women in general, and female college students in particular, to "turn the television off," but a multitude of studies have shown that television is not the only medium that misrepresents. The argument here is that through the critical viewing and analysis of shows like the ones mentioned in this chapter, televisions do not have to be turned off, and in fact serve as an epistemological tool. A university professor who blogs wrote an entry in 2005 called "Turn Off the TV Week." The assignment simply asked students to deprive themselves of a form of media for a week. The professor reported:

> They all HATED it, but learned just how saturated they are with media and how reliant they have habitually become on it. Students wrote about the sheer terror of actually hearing their car engines while they drove, or the frustrating horrors of not being able to play with their X-Boxes or the haunting sounds of other people's media that they couldn't escape from. Several admitted failure and gobbling up as much IM'ing and CD playing as they could after going half a day without them, like a smoker caving in to the cravings of a nicotine fix. I wouldn't say it changed their lives, but it really opened their eyes.[25]

Of the 55 Black female students that participated at workshop with me, almost all of them reported that *Gossip Girl* and *College Hill* were on their top-10 list of "favorite shows to watch." Next on the list was any variety of reality TV shows, particularly ones that had leading Black cast members, such as *Basketball Wives*, *Real Housewives of Atlanta*, and *Bad Girls*. Nielsen reported in 2006, that students watch 24.3 hours of television to which the professor's blog reported: "that's [TWICE] the amount of time the average full-time student sits in a class."[26] Considering these statistics, educators have to be conducive and adhesive to the breaking of stereotypes by including their pedagogy along with statistical data about what their students are doing outside of the classroom. If educators are presenting examples of misrepresentation of women on television (particularly Black women), they must also be very informed and aware about ways to empower students with the skills necessary to begin watching programs through critical examination. With the development of such critical skills, pre-college women of color in particular can begin deciphering what images accurately represent them, and college women can begin consuming better versions of representation while producing their own form of collegiate culture.

CHAPTER THREE

Making Black Studies Political

Although the Black Panthers and other Black Nationalist activists come alive in various Black Studies courses, and are again brought to life through readings about and by the original members of these organizations, students of Black Studies need further assistance in developing Black identity on campus. Colleges all around the nation saw a diverse set of student protests during the 1960s. Some were violent and many peaceful, but at the center of a countless number of these protests was the demand for an inclusive curriculum that represented a culturally diverse and culturally relevant set of knowledge (Black Studies). One major movement toward the creation of such a program was at San Francisco State University (SFSU) in 1968, as per the demand of student activists. Prior to the actual establishment of the Black Studies Department, the student activists demanded the following[1]:

1. That all Black Studies courses being taught through various other departments be immediately made part of the Black Studies Department, and that all the instructors in this department receive full-time pay.

Many relevant courses are still offered through various other disciplines and are not cross-listed with Black Studies departments. Furthermore, many of the public colleges have enormous quantities of part-time adjuncts, so many that they outnumber or rival the full-time faculty.

2. That there be a Department of Black Studies which will grant a Bachelor's Degree in Black Studies; that the Black Studies Department, the Chairman, faculty and staff have the sole power to hire faculty and control and determine the destiny of its department.

As you will see throughout this book, many programs remain at the minor level with equally minor requirements for completion.

3. That all unused slots for Black students from Fall 1968 under the Special Admissions Program be filled in Spring 1969.
4. That all Black students wishing to be admitted in Fall, 1969 [be admitted].
5. That twenty (20) full-time teaching positions be allocated to the Department of Black Studies.
6. That Dr. Helen Bedesem be replaced from the position of Financial Aids Officer, and that a Black person be hired to direct it, that Third World people have the power to determine how it will be administered.
7. That the California State College Trustees not be allowed to dissolve the Black programs on or off the San Francisco State College campus.

These and similar demands were made throughout many other schools all over the nation. The sounds of such protests, however, have now gone quiet and the protests are invisible on campus. At the threat of so many Black Studies programs and departments being closed down for one academic reason or another, students in this field of study continue to seek a home where they can be "themselves." Yet the very home has had trouble encouraging and teaching students just how they come to know themselves ontologically and racially, and ultimately politically. Housed in so many other college courses is the feeling of being the "other," or the "native informant" (bell hooks, 1994) as well a sense of displacement. One Black West Indian student said to me

> although we learn Mathematics in Trinidad and Guyana much differently than the westernized version, you would think this was the only way to learn it. Black people are invisible in Math (Philip, Black, Junior)

Although many Sociology and Anthropology classes make attempts at introducing a perspective on various topics on Black folk or Black identity, it is often limited to particular instances and productions of subcultures. Scores of Black students do not feel vocal or supported enough to raise a hand and introduce a "Black" point of view. Others do and are shut down by professors who are ill equipped to include a discussion about race or simply find no suitable opening for such a dialogue in the classroom, especially where Black students are outnumbered.

With this type of learning atmosphere, Black Studies begins to represent a variety of different things for students in this area of study and moves further away from its history in the creation of a new future. It begins to serve as a "home" within the college where they can share a physical and emotional space with people who "look like them" and who have encountered many of the same societal and academic experiences. The Black Studies Department also functions as a space where Black students can be allowed to be proud of their ideas, abilities, and common or even sometimes transnational/multicultural identities. It is a place, for many, where the classroom is seen as an extension of a larger social discussion on important topics. The educator responsible for such a political setting has a great breadth of knowledge to present but also has a large social responsibility to inculcate such an environment of political empowerment into their classroom.

While much of the threat against Black Studies still remains (closure of departments, lack of funding, low enrollment of students, the meshing of Black topics into existing and traditional departments), the political ideology of students has taken a major shift as well. Analyzed here over a period of 10 years, Black Studies students have a different set of foundational ideas at the workplace and ultimately at school. No longer is the urgent fight a demand for new or additional courses, nor is it to increase the diversity of its faculty hires. The students band together to fight national causes, none much related to the focus of Black Studies in particular. The pressure to obtain a four-year degree in four actual years has presented to the students what they deem "bigger issues." Students face not only the pressure of changes in curriculum and entrance exams to be accepted into "specialized" programs within their school but also tuition increases mid-semester, the search for part-time or full-time jobs, and personal obligations. Additionally, many students are also very attracted to the social function that school serves, and thus find it difficult to balance their academic responsibilities with their social invitations (both on and off campus). This is particularly true when networking as a practice is pushed very heavily by school administration.

Today, there is also an element of fear and individualism that did not seem to be present among the student activists of the 1960s. Perhaps, because some students are not supported by a Black Studies major at their particular school (as opposed to the offerings of minors, certificates and programs), they feel they are without institutional support to make demands.

> I can't afford to fight this fight. I have to graduate. If people want Black Studies, Puerto Rican Studies or even Ethnic Studies they have to join together. This group is too small, and everyone is too visible. You gotta get a large group so no one is left without back up. Suppose I get in trouble for being an agitator, you think anyone of these people are gonna back me

up so I can graduate? I have kids, I can't risk this. (Victoria, Puerto Rican/Black, Senior)

Such fears are not new, and this is not an isolated case example. In 1968, when the Black Student Union tried to recruit Black athletes on the SFSU campus, the athletes hesitated to participate for fear of retaliation from their coaches.

> When the athletes saw Black Student Union members stand up to the coaches, they began to realize that the coaches were not Gods. When the strike occurred, the athletes supported the strike by refusing to play (Africana Studies Department History, SFSU).

As students juggle the rigors of academics and outside-school issues, the fight for academic or racialized-academic equality seems to be the last issue on the list of how school is political. How Black Studies becomes political is identified in very disengaged ways. Teach-ins, along with sit-ins, were very popular in the 1960s, particularly among students of Black Studies. At the site where I spent years chronicling the functionality of Black Studies, teach-ins are limited because of scheduling conflicts and lack of space on campus, as well as poor marketing; sit-ins just do not make themselves into the lives of students. As one student told me when I first began working on this book,

> what will protesting do, when everyone still has to come back here [school] to get their degree? No one is going to walk out. No one will reject the school. The school will just find a replacement if we fight back (Megan, Black, Upper Senior)

Many of these students are goal oriented and like the idea of quick gratification. Thus, the idea of a teach-in or a sit-in seems like an additional task in hours not allotted to them for creative collectivism.

Students Then and Somewhat Now[2]

Over the course of several semesters, I began to consider the role of Black Studies among both the students I had been teaching and those I had direct access to through workshops I held for this project. I wanted to compare and contrast them to Black Studies students of the 1960s, to other students around the city that were pursuing undergraduate and graduate degrees in the field. In almost 10 years of close contact with students in Black Studies, I have had only two students who were majoring in the field, and, due to lack of space and offering at their home school, they ended up having to take classes all over their university's sister-schools through a consortium and electronic permit process. In addition, sometimes personal interest in particular courses offered at one and not another school drove students out of their registered institution and into classrooms in another borough. It was clear, that although the fight seemed to be at a temporary halt (as with the students quoted above), the desire and earnest interest in Black Studies were prevalent among many.

The students I talk about for this chapter and other sections of this book are those that were only given the outright option of pursuing a mere minor in Black Studies at their home school (which requires three unrelated courses in the field). Such students who wished to pursue a major in Black Studies were encouraged to pursue "ad-hoc degree programs," where they are given academic freedom and minimum guidelines to construct, create, and execute academic majors of their own creation. Over the years leading up to this book, I have held and observed several forums, panel discussions, student showcases, teach-ins, field trips, and late night discussions over internet instant messenger programs on issues dealing specifically with Black collegiate culture and Black Studies. Participants in these analysis groups worked tirelessly to identify and define some of the major issues they were encountering when it came to their academic pursuit of a bachelor's degree and issues they faced post-graduation.

A more recent discussion began with the topic of tuition (which was a major concern for students not receiving financial aid).[3] These students attending my workshop group were asked to compare their positions and concern with the students protesting massive tuition hikes organized by the National Union of Students in London (BBC News, 2010).[4] They found no common ground between themselves and the British students who were opposing the very same issue of academic financing. When asked about the breakdown of their Bursars receipts, the group of students sitting at my workshop could not identify more than half of the institutional acronyms on their bills. Yet they dutifully paid their bills either outright, by loans, or through financial aid.[5] During the workshop, it was discovered that within their tuition, there was a charge for "student activities fees" such as club memberships/functions, and gym services. More than half of the students in the workshop were not members of any of the clubs, nor did they have time to use the gym. A second charge on the bill was for "student printing." The students disclosed that whether or not they used all of the printing allotted to them in a semester (paid for at the beginning of the semester), the money or page allotment did not roll over to the subsequent semester, and there was no refund for unused paper. One student very proudly announced that she and many others had found clever ways to "beat the system." She went on to illustrate that when using the computer labs at the end of the semester, she and her friends printed out blank sheets of paper until her allotment ran out. She said she was determined not to give the school more than she had already paid: "they would not get my paper too!" (Angela, Black West Indian, Sophomore). Her peers cheered her idea, and undoubtedly that would be something they would try in the future semester. When the applause died down, there was some clear disgust towards the "blind payment" of tuition. Yet, the students felt there was no other choice. "If we want to go here, we have to pay it, otherwise, they'll [the school] just find someone else to replace us" (Angela, Black West Indian, Sophomore).

Analysis Group and Student Clubs

The students in the analysis group moved on to a discussion about Black Student clubs and campus organizations and their response or lack thereof to such issues (tuition, courses, pedagogical practices in their various classes, and Black Studies). Many of the Black student clubs and campus organizations were represented on school grounds through word-of-mouth membership and recruitment as well as through reputations as "fun clubs" to join (because of end of the semester parties). In 2003,[6] the Black student clubs made a rule that club presidents take a Black Studies class (sometimes more than one, depending on unwritten club rules). Club members were required to hold weekly events that focused on issues affecting Black Students on their campus in particular, but also off campus at other schools. With little or no institutional funds and support, these student clubs were a major presence on campus, recruiting Black students from various classes to join their organizations and increase their numbers. Although they did not wear uniform clothing, their clubrooms were reminiscent of what the Black Panther Party and Young Lords meeting-rooms had looked like. Their clubrooms were adorned with various African and West Indian flags, and the sounds of reggae and Hip Hop could be heard from far away. Some days were standing room only in their small spaces, but students did not mind sitting on top of one another, on tables, on the floor and on window sills. During this time, in their private clubrooms, the Black student organizations hosted political dialogues about race on campus. There was something brewing on campus, and it was all unraveling through dialogue in these clubrooms. Time seemed to take flight during many of the visits I made, and students could often be seen scrambling for their bags and still debating on their way towards their classes.

To continue the discussion and present students with a space to have this dialogue (not just with each other but with a faculty member present to facilitate the discussion), I designed "lunch-time lecture." Lunch-time lecture was held in my tiny adjunct office, isolated from the fulltime faculty members. Students in the class, as well as those participating in the analysis group (sometimes as many as 20 students crammed into the office), would chip in for lunch of the most unhealthy sort (student budgets) and spend close to two hours discussing race and their struggle to obtain their degrees. The students loved this space, and often tried to race to the adjunct office to make sure they got a space in the doorway if all the seats were gone. Through these early workshops I began working on a theoretical approach to identifying this type of pedagogy, which I now call *communal-class*. In this format, communal-class combines traditional classroom activities (such as the standard instruction and receiving of information), with cost-sharing for supplies, reading materials, and other benefits of communal learning. However, due to structural changes to core curriculum requirements, changes in faculty and departmental initiatives, low recruitment, ever-decreasing enrollment and retention of Black students (as well as Latino/a students), that very space that took such time to create has taken a significant blow. In fact, it has almost disappeared some nine years later.

There is no doubt that Black Studies remains as important to current students as it was to the students waging the war for inclusion in the 1960s, as well as the students I worked with for ten years ago, but the political agenda of many students has taken a significant turn. With sharp decreases in Black student enrollment, tuition hikes, strict rules, and streamlined policy initiatives, Black Studies as just a minor area of study (as opposed to a major) began to struggle to remain political for students. In fact, the disappearance of said programs and concentrations (as majors) is arguably what remains political about it.

Observed at an informal Black Studies forum were students who had never taken a single Black Studies course, although there was an interest. Participants declared:

1. The school did not require Black or Cultural Studies as part of the core curriculum, and as students held a main focus of trying to graduate in four years, they were not enticed to extend their time at the school by taking courses that did not allow them to keep on track.
2. They also suggested that they were not exposed to Black history/studies in high school and had hoped they would buy once they landed in college. But if they were not required to, they would not venture beyond their time and financial constraints.

The group was asked about significant writers in the field of Black Studies and their exposure to such Black thought in other fields (non–Black Studies classes). Key figures in Black Studies were named in hopes of collective recognition among the students (particularly students currently enrolled in Black Studies classes).

1. Notable Scholars: many had never read the works of W.E.B. Du Bois, Booker T. Washington, Manning Marable, Amiri Baraka, bell hooks, or Patricia Hill Collins.
2. Black Classic Literature: they knew *The Color Purple* was a musical on Broadway and a film with Whoopie Goldberg and Oprah, but did not know Alice Walker authored the book from which the film, and later the musical, were created.
3. Malcolm X: all the students around the table had read excerpts of the *Autobiography of Malcolm X* in a course taught by a single Black Studies professor at the university. They all recognized this professor, either through their friends or because they had taken multiple classes with him. The majority of the students confessed that they were unable to finish the autobiography but "caught up with the story" by way of Denzel Washington in his portrayal of Malcolm X in Spike Lee's film version.

Nevertheless, they had *all* seen *Training Day* and seemed outraged that Denzel Washington had won his Oscar for this film and not *Malcolm X*. The majority of the students at the forum barely recognized the names of important members of the Black Panthers but knew they were a major force for Black people "back then." Still, there was no immediate connection to the movement and what it means for Black Studies today.

When asked about their interest in Black Studies, the student response was quite diverse. Among some of their interests was

> to find other Black people on campus (Elijah, Black, Sophomore)

and, to see if Black Studies was reflective of what they saw on the television show *A Different World*. Inspired to create a "fun" space for Black students, the Black student organizations on campus developed the reputation and attribute of being "the party club." A few of the White students around the table admitted they joined the Black clubs because

> they have the best parties, with the better DJs (Mike, Polish, Junior).

An interesting note here about White students attending these open forums, workshops, and analysis groups is that, unless they were current students of mine, they were not directly invited by me. Rather, many of the Black students had invited their White friends. The sentiment among the younger White male students suggested that they took Black Studies classes because they either (1) liked to learn about "cultures" outside of their own, and (2) were looking for girls of color to date. From their disposition, attitude, and way of self, many of the White male student participants seemed to be ultimately searching for "credibility" among Black folks at the college. Although the Black participants were just college students like themselves, many White male students felt as though by hanging around them they would learn how to maneuver among women, while learning about "the code of the street" (Anderson, 1999).

Thus, among Blacks and Whites on campus, the Black clubs developed a reputation for hosting the best on- and off-campus bashes, with no real agenda—at least no politically or intellectually-based agenda (unless prompted by single militant students, guided by equally militant professors). Many of the clubs hosted parties and social events that included bar and lounge activities but did not host academic panel discussions or intellectually-based events in bulk after 2006. The analysis group suggested that one of the reasons they did not host intellectual or "smart" events was because of low attendance. They also suggested,

> If you want to get a good turnout, you have to trick the people into thinking it's a party, or a chill-session, so that they will come. Students don't want to attend more lectures outside of the class. (Joe, Black, Senior)

Of their functions, one of the most controversial was their end-of-year fashion show. The club that hosted this event was known and envied by other clubs for being awarded the biggest student club budget among all the clubs on campus. This event brought in some of the biggest entertainers, much to the protest by other student clubs, who had much less funding for their events and entertainers. This divide in financing of student groups created an animosity on campus that was hard to ignore, one that undoubtedly included a racial connotation. The Black students, who supported this event, defended themselves and their programming by claiming the show was cultural and gave their peers and the school a look at their identity outside of the classroom.

> Who knows more about our culture [West Indian] than we do? We're gonna wait for someone else to market this event and pretend like they know us? Even the University President comes to see our show. (Shawqueta, Black, Sophomore)

While this may be true, many other students protested the scantily-clad men and women that walked the runway at the fashion show (all students), the gyrating dances (by student participants), and rejected the notion that any of these activities were culturally representative of Black identity. More radical students felt the fashion show was a "meat market" that "set the race back" and perpetuated the stereotype that Black people best serve everyone on a stage, entertaining the masses.

Tepid resistance allowed the club to continue their fashion show tradition, with other groups losing ground in competing with such a popular event.

Although the school housed over 66 student organizations, both graduate and undergraduate (2010), only four clubs were available for Black students (not including three fraternity and sorority chapters that were either Black or Latino/a based). Simply by existing, these clubs serve an important function for Black students upon their arrival. Prior to college acceptances, they envisioned a place where Black students had not only a major social presence (based on the depictions in television shows about college life), but also equal footing within the realm of academics. Black students were shocked that television programming did not accurately portray their own academic experiences. Even more daunting was the encounter with other Black students on campus who did not share their political ideologies. For many of these students, Black Studies was the space presented to them as a relief from their more "strenuous" courses in Math, Science, Business, Law, or Pre-Med. Many of the non-black and non-Latino/a students took Black Studies courses as electives and thought the titles of some of the courses were

> more interesting than other choices we could have made, such as Women Studies, Asian Studies, and Jewish Studies, or basic Ethnic Studies. What is Ethnic Studies anyway? (Jaleesa, Black, sophomore).

A handful of Black West Indian and Black Caribbean students felt isolated from Black Studies because there were no course offerings on Guyana, Trinidad, Jamaica, and other places within the non-Spanish-speaking Caribbean. Errol declared,

> I'm not American Black and I'm not from African, so I'm not African American. This school has a West Indian Club, and all of us meet and get together there, but what about the classes? You mean to tell me none of the faculty is from any of our islands? (Errol, Black, Senior)

For these students, it was difficult to associate themselves with an all-encompassing Black identity, because their cultural heritage and racial makeup draw from a variety of places outside of the United States. Thus, they found it difficult to join particular clubs that did not represent them both racially and academically and ended up creating their own club. This led to much animosity among American Black students who felt that Black West Indian students thought of themselves "better than" American Blacks. Other students felt that they were just "regular Black" and thus being part of any Black population presented the possibility that the courses at the school and the clubs on campus may represent them to a greater and more accurate degree.

Black Pedagogues

Cultural politics began to rear its head when students discussed the racial makeup of faculty members offering Black Studies and/or Black-related courses. The majority of the students were uncomfortable with White professors and provided examples of why: one student reported that his White male professor would preface any conversation about civil rights, civil unrest, protest, and slavery by asking the students not to persecute him because he is White; in turn the professor was quite apologetic for American atrocities against people of color (slavery), and reminded them that although he too is White, he had no hand in such a gross crime against humanity. As the student revealed,

> He would stand in front of the class and say sorry every time he recounted a moment in slavery. Very embarrassing for him and us and the rest of the White people up in that room. (Jeremiah, Black, Senior)

At the above statement, a thunderous roar of laughter erupted from all the Black students in the workshop room. Another student reported that his professor, during a lecture and seminar discussion on civil rights, was brought to tears recounting lynching and hosing of African Americans during the 1960s Civil Rights movement. The professor had to abruptly adjourn class. While many students in that particular class were reminded of how moved they were by such a sincere display of hurt, others felt embarrassed for the professor, and what appeared to be the recounting of their (the Black students') racial history.

> Yo, maybe he was really feelin' it. You don't know. Maybe he was there when it happened. Was he old? Why didn't you ask him why he was crying? I would have asked him. That sounds deep. (Joe, Black, Senior)

Another Black female student responded to Joe:

> Why are you defending him? He should be sorry, it was his people that put us in the predicament we're in. We're busy killing each other now, we don't know what we're doing. (Jessica, Black, Senior)

Jessica's statement brought a chilly hush to the room, and brought all of the earlier laughter into a complete halt. Jessica was clearly enraged by Joe's support of the White professor's emotional breakdown and felt immediately betrayed by his comment being shared in public. Even Joe was brought to silence but didn't seem embarrassed. He just shrugged his shoulders at me, as I ferociously tried to take down every single note on my pad.

With subjects like Black Studies, no matter that some believe we are now in a post-racial society because of our biracial president, Barack Obama, the truth is, we aren't and race still matters, maybe even more so now. Yet in opposition, the organic intellectual is trained to think by interpreting experience, or hermeneutics and thus applies consumed knowledge to those very lived experience (race) thus, producing new forms of knowledge. Race, gender, socioeconomics, and ethnic history are central parts of one's learning experience, particularly at predominantly White institutions or places where subjects like Black Studies are minor components of the degree program.

Many of my own undergraduate history classes were with White professors, who often related Black history with slavery as its starting point. The pressure to represent Black identity in specific classrooms with professors who deem students as racially-other simplifies and begins to deconstruct the humanity of the student. By identifying single students as representatives of a topic and/or subject, educators begin to contribute to the construction of a "native informant" (hooks, 43). In classrooms heavily populated by White students and professors alike, the pressure on individual Black students to represent an idea of "Blackness" or Black identity leads to isolation and perhaps embarrassment, should the topic be less than flattering. Many of my Black undergraduates have stated that this weight of representation, particularly if the professor is White, exposes them as "militant" and oftentimes "angry." Additionally, my Black students have stated that they always have a racial perspective in all of their classes, because for them, they cannot initially see things in any other way. Race is such a central part of their identity that their understanding(s) of the information as well as the construction of the class, and their relationship to the professor, are always either racially or culturally infused.

At the various universities reviewed for this project, many of the "affiliated" professors teaching in Black Studies programs have "traditional" homes like Sociology, Anthropology, History, and/or English. There are fewer and fewer faculty members with degrees in Black Studies teaching in the field—it is not their home department.

> We cannot afford to have historians, qua historians, psychologists, qua psychologists, political scientists, qua political scientists, communicationists, qua communicationists speaking for our discipline simply because they found a job in African or African American Studies. It is a measure of our institutional weakness, not our intellectual weakness (Asante, 2005, 45).

The disconnect in professors to Black Studies and their traditional departments or area of research (not having to do with Black Studies) creates an increase in student anxiety and also creates less of a likelihood to pursue the field in a graduate program, as there is no successful model they can quickly cite.

Teaching

Teaching courses at a public college means teaching a rich population of young, multiracial, multilingual, and economically diverse students, who all exude energy for delivery of information, especially if that information will help them graduate, on time, without too much distraction or "extracurricular" work. At schools that place a heavy focus in retaining students for "professional" majors (such as Business, Law, and/or Pre-Med), Black Studies becomes an elective in degree requirements, in attitude, and in faculty recruitment. Black students majoring in "professional fields of study" at public institutions place great pressures on themselves in addition to the university pressures they face as they compete against graduates of more well-known schools (particularly Ivy League) for a decreased number of opportunities in corporate America. The community from which many of the students hail remains their place of residence but is not one to which they intend to return after graduation. That was a particular goal of the creation of Black Studies: community partnerships, community building, and re-strengthening of dilapidating neighborhoods (Stevens, 2003).

> There is a more serious and correlating debt that all of us must pay upon re-entry to the real world. When we leave academia with our degrees safely tucked under our arms, we should realize that our accumulated skills and our individual concern can change the lives of a community or a child (Owens, 42).

Important to note here is the Black faculty member who encourages service learning opportunities and projects that are steeped in the history of Black Studies and involves students in hands-on learning alongside members of struggling communities. Yet, many members of Black Studies programs are trained in traditional fields of academia and use the community as a research base for their own work as opposed to involving students and integrating this very involvement into the course curricula. As pedagogues in the field, we come from a variety of academic backgrounds as mentioned above. Many teach Black Studies from a variety of perspectives whether it is a racial perspective or not and whether we are limited to Black Studies courses or otherwise.

At many urban and public undergraduate institutions, the presentation of the Black Studies professor is of utmost importance to students, particularly the Black and White students. Latino/a students seemed to be comfortable with any educator teaching Black Studies, but felt uncomfortable with a non-Latino/a teaching Latino/a Studies. Before my own classes became "popular," my surname would dissuade students from registering. Through private conversations and later at research workshop(s) meetings, they shared with me that they were expecting an older White female, and found themselves "pleasantly surprised" that I was the total opposite. Some would wonder whether or not it really matters who is teaching the course, as long as they have a command of the material, a genuine expertise and interest in the field. These same students have gone even further stating that they would not be comfortable taking Black Studies courses at a predominantly White institution because the authenticity of the material would be lost in the mechanical approach to pedagogy (from what they have come to stereotype as "Ivy League education" and its educators). For these students, White professors regardless of gender (which is important to them in other areas of study, such as Women Studies) would have to then "prove" themselves and again prove that they actually care about the subject, in order to get student attention in the classroom, and be classified as "authentic."

In the Fall of 2010, 35 Black students participated in a lunch-time workshop about race and professors, where I posed the question: "are you comfortable taking a Black Studies class with a professor who is White or not Black?" Of the 35 students:

> 15 students responded that they were not comfortable
> 12 students were comfortable
> Six students stated that they didn't care who was teaching, and
> Two students did not respond to the question at all.

Of 35 Black students who participated (this number would also reflect a traditional number of students in a Black Studies elective course), the uncomfortable students outweighed the comfortable students and the students who didn't have an opinion. The post-racial theory, particularly in college classes, among these Black students, has proven false.

It is not uncommon to find many young White instructors and/or professors teaching courses in Black Studies, but their pursuit of an open and communicative dialogue about Black Studies falls on stereotypes that s/he may be "appropriating" racial and cultural movements and processes. A recent article in the *Los Angeles Times* reviewed two White professors, a veteran educator and a newcomer to the field of Black Studies. Each understands their position as "members of the majority [...] in a profession where [he's] the minority" (Trice, 2009, 20). Both professors profiled in the article are from private institutions. Students that I have worked closely with have gone on to explain that it would be harder for a White professor to fail them (Black and Latino/a students), because they cannot gauge the experiences talked about in the classroom, unless all pedagogy and distributed material are strictly from a "textbook."

> Sometimes it's better to have a white professor for Black Studies. How is [s]he gonna fail me, when I'm Black and we're talking about Black Studies? You can't compare experience to a textbook. They would be too scared to fail Black students, so this is an easy pass (Jacob, Black, Sophomore)

According to these students, having a professor who represents the discussed population (Black or Brown) in many ways adds to their learning experience, and also adds difficulty in any attempt to slack. Students associate race, and sometimes gender as well, to the relationship they have to Black Studies and the professor who is in charge of information delivery. Ideally, they want the educator to be of the traditional intellectual population (Bernard-Carreño, 2010),[7] complete with a PhD, but still have many of the organic intellectual qualities in order to relate better to the students themselves.

> In many instances, students have decided that blackness, publication of some kind dealing with the black experience regardless of its nature and quality, loud and uncompromising allegiance to the black revolution as they understand it, and willingness to serve exclusively the needs of the black student population are the basic qualifications. These students insist that no white person is qualified to teach any subject dealing with the black experience (Ford, 591).

The point here is to indicate that this understanding of the structure of Black Studies leaves these students with a sense of needing and still wanting. Without accurate representation in the class by the professor (regardless of race) at the university-level and post-graduation, students continue to simply "just pass" their Black Studies classes with a short-term interest. Retaining and re-using information through the production of "indigenous knowledge" (Kincheloe, 3) in a classroom that does not elaborate on hermeneutical approaches or ontological frameworks of learning, Black and Latino/a students decrease their desire to pursue the topic any further. To be disconnected from the learning experience(s) of our Black Studies students depletes our purpose as pedagogues in the field, and thus we run the risk as we did back in the 1960s of non-existence.

> This lesson and this apprenticeship must come, however, from the oppressed themselves and from those who are truly in solidarity with them.

As individuals or as peoples, by fighting for the restoration of their humanity they will be attempting the restoration of true generosity. Who are better prepared than the oppressed to understand the terrible significance of an oppressive society? Who suffer the effects of oppression more than the oppressed? Who can better understand the necessity of liberation? They will not gain this liberation by chance but through the praxis of their quest for it, through their recognition of the necessity to fight for it. And this fight, because of the purpose given it by the oppressed, will actually constitute an act of love opposing the lovelessness which lies at the heart of the oppressors' violence, lovelessness even when clothed in false generosity (Freire, 2000, 133).

Much of the controversy or concern surrounding White instructors of Black Studies is the worry about whether the instructor has an authentic passion for the topic or whether or not they are "ripping off" Black history, in what scholar Mark Christian has deemed "opportunists in Black Studies" (Christian, 2007). Additionally, there is also trepidation around Whites researching Blacks, Black culture, and the Black experience and producing voyeuristic works where they are not held accountable by other Black scholars.[8] Many Black scholars echo the sentiments of Black students and Black citizens all over the nation—or those that feel uncomfortable with White professors teaching Black Studies.

In 2009, *The Chicago Tribune* created an online forum, similar to the public student workshop I had in the Fall of 2010, which posed the same kind of question: "Can white professors effectively teach in a discipline that requires such an immersion into black culture?"[9] Once the question was published on the *Tribune*'s site, the responses came pouring in. The counterargument that has been long presented, "should White professors be the only ones to teach European history?" was plastered all over the forum. Forgetting that many Europeans are also Black, these types of comments went unaddressed. However, many contributors to the question, stated their concern for the hiring of White Black Studies professors as a cloak to getting rid of Black (or of-color) Black Studies professors who were later or at some point during their teaching careers and for whatever reason, seen as "untenurable." Another contributor suggested that this replacement of Black professors has been a historical and recurring practice at various schools, and thus this is a new form of such a practice. Historically, and as detailed in later chapters in this book, the demands for Black Studies programs all over the nation came with strict demands for the immediate hiring of Black professors in those programs, along with giving existing Black professors tenure in other departments. Some see the influx of young White professors of Black Studies as a way to rid of emerging and seasoned Black scholars alike. Many others on the site commented that Black Studies being taught by White professors would "white wash" political and social issues that create discomfort for the professor and that productions of Black culture would essentially be "hijacked" by professors who aren't Black. A handful believed that there was no link between experience and conveying information.

As in my own undergraduates and the students who participated in the Black Studies workshops with me, much of the other comments at this initial informal forum were based on pedagogical activities in the class that were not necessarily representative of the history of Black Studies. Students recounted that professors taught from their own area of expertise as opposed to presenting a wider breadth of knowledge in the field of Black Studies. Students found it odd to learn Black Studies from traditional textbooks that cost them over $100 and had extremely low re-sale values (if any at all). Many were disgruntled that these texts, although assigned and listed at the bookstore as "required," were never used in class, even though assigned readings appeared on examinations throughout the semester. A handful of these students were also disgruntled by the course title and descriptions not being consistent with actual course content. While the critical questioning of course titles and class content (including pedagogical practices) created a draining environment for them, the students did not know what to do with their complaints. It was clear that the tradition of Black resistance had not fully died or disappeared among them, but the students did not see an immediate need for such action at their school. They felt helpless to some extent and not supported by an abundance of Black faculty, with slight exceptions of one or two faculty members. Neither were they so inclined to participate in any activity that would protest sister schools that engaged in other acts of inequality and bias. They were not prepared to engage in research that would present a solid Black Studies curriculum at other schools nor to perhaps use that to make demands at their own school. Many did not feel that protesting any of the above issues would be valued, and there would be no administrative response, other than removal from school, which no one wanted to risk. After examination of these issues, the analysis group was asked whether they thought college students had the power to effect social change at their schools and within their larger communities. Of the 100 asked, the following answered yes:

20 Blacks
Four Whites
Four Latino/as
Eight Asians (combined with Southeast Asian) students
64 students avoided the question completely.

Offered among the suggestions of "how students can effect change," the four White students suggested:

1. Teaming up with politicians (although they too are problematic).
2. Living through experience instead of what one is told.
3. Passion and organization required among the students.
4. Numbers. If there are enough people to support a cause, they can make a difference.

The 20 Black students suggested:

1. Educated minds are able to come up with current solutions.
2. Engaging in dialogue and breaking through propaganda.
3. Using voice and armed with current and future information.
4. Life experience.
5. Bringing awareness to break down stereotypes.
6. Working at afterschool organizations to help children.
7. Setting standards among themselves.
8. By utilizing the space of student clubs.
9. Doing whatever they can to address issues.
10. Openly discussing issues faced by college students as well as society.
11. Unity.
12. Self-awareness of other cultural groups.
13. Being more active in one's own community.
14. Protests and boycotts.

The Asian/Southeast Asian students suggested:

1. Mentoring
2. Trying to work with diverse groups to understand various cultures.
3. School events that teach how to address issues they face.
4. Collective action.

The Latino/a students suggested:

1. Becoming some of the most influential people in society.
2. Communication.
3. Pushing each other to become successful.

As the handful of above suggestions illustrate, the students for the most part believed they could effect change, but it would have to done as a collective. Not one student believed they could lead a change movement on their own, and none suggested that they would be the starting point for such a movement. One student responded:

I am a coward, and if it takes a revolution to make change, I will join, but I won't lead it or start it." (Jonathan, Asian, Junior).

When the statistics and percentages of Black students at their college were examined, none of the students seemed visibly bothered by the low percentage of Black student enrollment at their school (11 percent of the student body at the time this chapter was written) as compared to other schools in their city. However, the students did start to notice that they were not seeing many Black students on campus, in their classes, entering/exiting the buildings, and in the cafeteria. They admitted that they had not considered the political implication of being ranked the "most diverse school in the nation," yet they also had one of the lowest Black student enrollments in their entire hub of schools and sister-schools alike.

At the core of Black activism has been the access or lack thereof to quality standards of higher education.[10] Yet, the variables of such a higher education remain in silent questions and tranquil opposition. With all types of policy initiatives being presented and put into place without student influence, students are driven by the pressures to complete their "core" curriculum requirements without hesitation and without too much interruption. That is not to say that many of them see Black Studies as an interruption, but the attitudes and rationales for fighting for Black Studies have somewhat been altered and have been severely quieted.

Policy Initiatives

In 2004, the City University of New York instituted the "Black Male Initiative" (BMI) order to attract, enroll, and retain more Black male students in college and to help improve the jarring statistics that suggest their failure during and after high school. Their task force reported the following findings:

> According to the Schott Foundation for Public Education, in 2000–01, the four-year high school graduation rate for black males in New York City was 31%. The nationwide college graduation rate for black men in 2003 was 34%, according to *The Journal of Blacks in Higher Education*. New York City census data for 2000 indicates that only 55.2% of black males aged 16–64 had jobs. New York State Department of Criminal Justice Services reports that, in 2003, the arrest rate for black males per 100,000 was 18,575, in contrast to white males at 4,480.[11]

Although the BMI policy and program initiative is both a critical and politically direct response to the under-enrollment of Black men in college, the program also encourages its students to pursue degrees in fields other than Black Studies. The BMI taskforce stated their nine major recommendations for programming purposes[12] as follows:

1. Provide strong university leadership on the challenges facing black youth and men;
2. Strengthen the school-to-college pipeline to enable many more black male students to move into higher education;
3. Increase admission and graduation rates at CUNY colleges;
4. Improve teacher education to prepare professionals for urban education;
5. Improve employment prospects for black males;
6. Contribute to the reduction of the incarceration rate for black men;
7. Establish an Institute for the Achievement of Educational and Social Equity for Black Males;
8. Involve experts in the implementation of the recommendations; and
9. Establish benchmarks and hold Colleges accountable for implementing these recommendations.

These nine recommendations are extremely important to the overall presentation of the BMI and central to the overall goal of recruiting and retaining Black male youth on college campuses. However, it is arguable that the program could also be housed within a Black Studies department. The Black Studies department ideally can accomplish each of the recommendations above with ease, passion, and intellectual rigor. There is no better department to house such a program to keep the tradition of assisting the Black community in producing some of its best academic scholars and traditional intellectuals. However, the reality illustrates that at some schools the BMI is near invisible, and the Black students enrolled in the program are not strongly connected to the Black Studies Department(s) other than taking one class.

At one participating school, the young men take a single or perhaps two courses in Black Studies, but only one semester is required—the second class would be solely at their discretion. They generally take their Black Studies requirement during the summer (housed at the college of their BMI enrollment) of their junior or senior year in high school. Unless the students keep in touch after their college course right through their high school graduation, and then college life, the Black Studies faculty member may never see them again in any of their classes. The young men tend to be shadowed by their BMI program advisors and not by any faculty member responsible for representing Black Studies. To not house these young Black men and offer them a mentor and mentoring program through Black Studies departments is a gross administrative, collegiate, and leadership blunder—particularly since programs like these were created to circumvent prison, unemployment, and high dropout rates. When the Civil Rights movement spread to the SFSU student body, it was those very students who organized and won jobs for Blacks in the towns around San Francisco. Why then wouldn't programs geared for Black men be housed in the department of Black Studies, where faculty members trained in such fields could offer a shadow process to these young men as they navigate through and ultimately complete their degrees in any field?

> A major part of this effort to recognize fully the African American men on campus must be an attempt to learn about the particular sociocultural characteristics of this student population itself. To be effective in assisting African American men's matriculation, one must have a reasonable understanding of that population (Cuyjet, 2006).

Robert Allen's article "Politics of the Attack on Black Studies" suggests that during the 1960s, the entire atmosphere of Blacks in higher education had a protest pulse. There was an underlying sense of urgency among Black students to be inculcated into the general curriculum of a variety of schools (private and public colleges). He lists two major reasons for such a pulse during the 1960s:

1. For the first time masses of Black students became involved in the struggle of educational change; and
2. It became widely recognized that not only were Black students and teachers largely excluded from American higher education, but the totality of the Black experience was not to be found in curricula of the vast majority of colleges and universities.

Some 40 years later, much is still left to be desired and revamped. Where Allen claims that Black experience was not found in curricula circa 1960s, it is still remains invisible at many institutions, and at many others only samplings of such a perspective are included. While Black Studies still provides some sort of relic of political positioning in the academic establishment, the anxious pulse with an underbelly of protest has seen a major decline among those who really can benefit from it.

Why Black Studies?

Using the Black Studies analysis and workshop groups, 100 students were asked why they had chosen Black Studies as opposed to offerings in Women's Studies,

Latino/a Studies, Jewish Studies, Asian Studies, Sociology or Anthropology courses based on race (or people of color) or courses generally listed under "Ethnic Studies." The students had no idea that many of the other departments that represented marginalized populations sprang from the historical protest and eventual establishing of Black Studies departments across the nation. The students were then asked why they registered for Black Studies:

WHY REGISTER FOR BLACK STUDIES?	BLACK	WHITE	LATINO/A	ASIAN	BIRACIAL/OTHER
Personal Interest	25	2	5	3	2
Required for Major	12	4	6	5	2
Unsure	6	1	1	0	1

A total of 25 students skipped the question all together, later indicating that they were all together unsure of why they were taking the course and felt underprepared to answer the question. Knowing now some of the ways in which they felt about their own varied interest(s) in Black Studies, the analysis group was then asked "How important is Black Studies in the college setting?" The responses to this question were articulated in the following ways:

HOW IMPORTANT IS COLLEGE?	BLACK	WHITE	LATINO/A	ASIAN	OTHER
Very. Should be a major	20	1	3	6	2
Somewhat. Minors are just as acceptable	13	6	5	4	4
Not at all. Black Studies should not be on its own	0	0	0	0	0

From the results above, it is interesting to look at the answers based within the racial groups as individual groups. Although more Black students were part of the analysis group, they were almost equal in their position about the importance of Black Studies. Also interesting to note here, more Asians were in support of Black Studies as a major than Latino/a students and students who identified as "other."

Overall, these students had a variety of elective course choices. However, Black Studies is not a direct course choice: it is one made by default, as the actual core requirement is to fulfill a "cultural course." Thus, Black Studies is offered under an all-encompassing bracket that competes with several other topics in this marginalized camp. In reviewing the courses available to the students in the analysis group that would fulfill the "cultural" requirement, the following were retrieved by a central registration system:

BLACK STUDIES: INTRO—this was taught in two sections in one semester by two different professors with very different discipline backgrounds. Neither section was offered during the daytime hours; rather, were both offered to evening students only. Additionally, because two different professors offered this particular course, each course had a different theme, and no cohesive structure. Second, neither of the two professors was in communication with the other about their course, students, or materials used. Only one professor held a degree in Black Studies. The other was a part-time replacement.

RACIST EXPRESSIONS—this course, not offered every semester, fills the "introductory" course requirement in the field of Black Studies. Problematically, this course is a different introduction than an actual "Introduction to Black Studies" course, where the material is historical and presents a broad and important set of ideas and information. Students in this area of study can take either of these two courses, as opposed to taking them both. In addition, dependent upon who is teaching these two specific courses, the information may overlap at some point in the semester, thus appearing to the student as repetitive instruction. Much of this feeling of repetition in Black Studies as a minor or certificate program dissuades students from pursuing the topic further.

BLACK CHILDREN—In eight years, this course has only been taught by a single professor who aims to change the syllabus, assignments and course readings every semester to keep the material fresh for a variety of students. No other professor in eight years has taught this course nor offered a companion or comparable course.

HISTORY OF BLACK ECONOMICS—is one of the more popular courses, taught by a veteran Black Studies professor of the department through which it is offered. The course also keeps up with contemporary topics in Black economic development and thus does not repeat in instruction, which increases its visibility to Black Studies students. Students who are not minoring in Black Studies have been known to register for this class.

ANGLOPHONE CARIBBEAN LIT—This course was not specifically offered through the Department of Black Studies; rather, a few seats were distributed to the Black Studies Department for cross-listing and cross-registration. The course was also not housed in the Black Studies Department, and thus not every member of the Black Studies faculty was eligible to teach it in any given semester. In addition, the course was heavily advertised by the department where it was housed, as opposed to being also advertised in Black Studies.

RACIAL AND INTERNATIONAL INEQUALITIES—This course allowed seats from other departments throughout the school in order to attract a wider student base. Although a major advertising attempt, the first day of class yielded mostly students from Sociology and Anthropology, who were mostly non-Black.

SPECIALIZATIONS IN BLACK STUDIES—These "specializations" had no detailed course description through its online presence/bulletin, other than suggesting the course will ultimately provide opportunities to focus on specific issues in the field of Black Studies from a variety of academic perspectives (Online Bulletin, 2010). These courses are taught from the expertise of the professor teaching the course, who will also design and direct the course without consultation of the larger faculty body or any such curriculum committee. There are limitations as to how many of these courses may be offered in specific departments during a single semester, and for Black Studies, it is oftentimes limited to three total, unless it is in competition with Latino Studies specialized classes. Courses are offered on a first-come first-serve basis, as opposed to faculty rotating the opportunity among themselves.

CIVIL RIGHTS—This course was also housed within the school's History department, and a few seats were allotted to Black Studies registrants, but because the class (similar to other classes both listed and unlisted here) is not offered out of the Black Studies Department, Black Studies faculty members cannot teach them directly. They may integrate the unit in their own classes.

IDENTITY—This course considers the "authenticity" of racial identification but is not solely housed in Black Studies. Students of Sociology and Anthropology, as well as other departments, have seats available to them.

LATIN AMERICAN & CARIBBEAN YOUTH—This course was cross-listed with Latino/a Studies and Sociology and does not centralize around Black Studies nor include discourse on the Black members of the Caribbean or Latin America.

Since Black Studies is offered solely as a minor and/or certificate program, there is no real shaping of a Black Studies identity or a concentrated consciousness for students. This is particularly true for those who participated in the Black Studies forum in the previously listed suggestions. Neither collectively nor individually did they have a Black identity that was steeped in academic tradition, as opposed to a larger individual intellectual pursuit of college degrees in various subjects. Students participating in Black Studies classes in this venue of randomized (or "potpourri," as it is called throughout this book) course offerings, are considering threads of the topic that are not necessarily connected to a larger focus of Black Studies as a serious body of intellectual work and academic production of knowledge. The political impact of these courses depends on the individual instruction of each class, the professor instructing, and the weight of the materials assigned. With this type of structure, students have to really pursue additional and outside-the-classroom knowledge in order to demand a stronger set of courses that represent a cohesive focus on Black Studies. It is even more imperative at schools where the majority of students are non-Black, and where some students are not comfortable with identifying as "Black," due to negative connotations of "Blackness" that are not being aggressively discussed in classrooms.

Introductory Black Studies courses also have to be quite present in core curriculum, and required of every student, not just those who are interested. In the introductory courses offered at one of the schools studied in this particular analysis, there are no classes on the Caribbean, West Indies, non–Spanish-speaking South America (such as Guyana), nor specific parts of Africa (although varyious courses on Africa in its entirety are offered, they are not offered every semester). Thus, there is no real historical introduction to people of color, as there is no cumulative ending.

To pursue a minor in Black Studies as per the students in the analysis group, at their particular college, there is one very concentrated seminar that is a requirement (offered at the senior level and after successful completion of any of the two courses listed above). However, these seminars are *also* taken by students who have been pursuing minors in Latino/a Studies, and who have never taken a single Black Studies class. While a collective identity of people of color and historical struggle is central to the life of either Black or Latino/a Studies if students have never taken courses outside of their singular study (Black or Latino/a as opposed to taking classes in both disciplines), it is simply the luck of the draw as to what type of instruction they will receive during seminar. Students from Black Studies may end up with a professor who has only taught classes in the Latino/a Studies discipline, and thus instead of the seminar providing a space for senior-level discussion on a concentrated topic, the discussion broadens and expands to inculcate another population whom they may never have studied or been academically introduced to. It appears as an introduction to unfamiliar students and a repetition to senior-level learners. What ends up happening here is the dislocation of knowledge production and thus another potpourri of important racial topics as a consumption of knowledge. There is no closure to Black Studies in this format, as there are only three classes required to fulfill a minor at this particular school, one being the senior seminar.

These are just a few of the reasons why Black Studies, in its historically political state and nature, needs to be an integral part of college core curricula, with strategic plans and critical curriculum construction inclusive of a wide array of voices.

While the current nature of Black Studies has changed and will include more contemporary politics of said topic in the future, the history remains strong. But it can, by all means, lose its connection to students of Black Studies if these courses are not offered widely. The introduction to the *African American Studies Reader*, edited by Nathaniel Norment Jr. (2007), offers a snapshot of the history of African American Studies and ideally what could be used for current and future department course offerings (even at the minor level). What the introduction in this text presents can assist in department and program creation, construction, and global strengthening. Norment includes Ancient Egypt or Kmt and Egypt's educational system or the "Egyptian Mystery System" (EMS) as a potential starting point, stating that EMS has been argued by scholars as "not only a blueprint for curriculum but can also help aid in the overall organization of the discipline itself."[13] The rest of the curriculum ideas are as follows:

> The American Negro Academy (Pre–1900 establishments)
> Intellectual Foundations (1900–1930)
> Historically Black Colleges & Universities Course Offerings (1930–1955)
> Social and Political Movements (1955–1970)
> Questions, Crisis & Criticism (1970–1985)
> Institutionalization (1985–2000)

After these six starting points (that should be primarily housed in Black Studies departments), more contemporary topics and subtopics within the six above should be offered to students for a broader range of knowledge. What many schools fail to see is that Black Studies and other topics of indigenous knowledge offer students a well-rounded education and training in human experience and communication. Post-graduation, these students have some type of entryway in learning how to effectively interact with diverse populations. As we move into a more diverse society, and schools that diversity, simply offering a potpourri of Black Studies classes is a disservice. Students are not being given the tools to aggressively engage in self-discovery without academic compromise, and some are not properly equipped to voyage out into the world of external knowledge to ask critical questions of themselves and of those responsible in educating them. How do you know what answers you are getting if you cannot formulate the question to which you seek such answers?

Potpourri courses tap the interest of students who wish to learn more about Black Studies, but without a cohesive program, the students are left with even more questions and limited training on how to seek out information and answers on their own. Many Black Studies minor programs do not offer courses on methodology in Black Studies. Where there was a methodology course offered, there were no courses leading up in content to methodological research because of the sprinkling of topics such as the ones discussed earlier in the chapter. In a review of course offerings in Black Studies, SFSU originally offered:

> Introduction to Black Studies
> Introduction to Black Psychology
> Black Involvement in Scientific Development
> Black Diaspora
> Economics of the Black Community
> Research Methods and Fieldworks in Black Studies

In addition to these offerings for the Black Studies core curriculum, students had to choose 12 units in any one of the three emphasis blocks: (1) Black Humanities Emphasis, (2) Black Behavioral & Social Sciences, and (3) Aesthetics Emphasis. Today, there are 56 courses offered through the Africana Studies department at SFSU, which students can use to make up their major or minor.[14] One could argue that given SFSU's history, their department has seen continuous growth.

In 1971, William D. Smith suggested constructing Black Studies programs around the following thematic programs: Africa, Arts and Humanities, Civil Rights, Economics, Education, English, General (such as: Black Utopia, Black Community Health, and Propaganda and the Black Nation), Government, History, Independent Study, Language, Law, Mathematics and Statistics, Music, Oral History, Other Cultures, Philosophy, Political Science, Psychology, Radio & TV, Religion, Science, Sociology, Speech, and Urban [Studies].[15] Following this list were suggestions of courses within the thematic structure that were representative of the subject heading. Although Smith's suggestions are a bit dated, including his idea of a course on "The Black Ghettos and Urban Spatial Form," one public college in New York currently offers the equivalent: "Selected Social Problems of the Ghetto." Many of Smith's suggestions are still replicated in today's Black Studies curricula at a variety of public institutions. Although terminologies that are representative of people, places, and events have since been updated, many school curricula have made no forceful effort to revamp the wording and descriptions of the classes they offer to their entire student population. Thus, at many schools, Black Studies is still being introduced by the history of slavery.

At a different public college in New York (from the analysis group school), the minor in Black Studies requires 18 credits in the field (equivalent to six classes). There are two required courses: (1) African Heritage and the Afro-American Experience, and (2) African Heritage and the Caribbean-Brazilian Experience. The rest of the credit requirements can be selected from Black World Development, Business, Science & Technology, African American Society, Latin American and

Caribbean Cultures, Special Topics, and Independent Studies. There are also offerings under "Intermediate Courses" which include a practicum course where students conduct academic and research work within "the community." A program such as this is more likely to keep within the traditional origins of Black Studies programs and thus continue the strength of retaining students and creating an important and militant presence on their campus among students and administration alike.

Norment suggests four main purposes[16] of Black Studies. In review of these, I will also present additional purposes for schools that do not offer majors in Black Studies. He suggests:

1. To analyze, produce, investigate, and disseminate knowledge about African people.
2. To involve and incorporate the content, ideologies, and methodologies of African American Studies in all aspects of the community.
3. To prepare undergraduate and graduate students with knowledge, skills, and paradigms to analyze critical factors which affect African people in America.
4. To identify issues and problems African Americans face and to provide leadership and solutions to resolve them.

The work of the critical educator who serves to reinforce the historical tradition of Black Studies while incorporating its contemporary features and functions is even more important when in a position to offer only limited amounts of courses. That is, the analysis, production, investigation, and dissemination of knowledge of people of color cannot be done in one course and cannot be completely discussed in three courses. This would require that the introductory course at a school that offers only a minor in Black Studies present students with the tools effective for such examination and later instruction on how to use those very tools. If this is considered one of four major purposes for Black Studies, in keeping with the political legacy of such a field of study, this task cannot be done in a single class but must offer itself as a reoccurring theme throughout a longitudinal study.

Second, incorporation of content that deals with ideologies, methodologies, and community investigation must also be part of a more-than-one-class offering. Since the evolution of Black Studies, not only has the politics of these kinds of departments changed significantly, along with its rebellious leaders both of the organic and traditional intellectual campus, and community freedom fighters, but the students have also changed to a great extent. By not offering a cohesive program of study, and no major in Black Studies, many students have begun to disassociate themselves with "the community." Many have even distanced themselves from their own community, and suggest that they must "be on" before they can "put other people on" (Eric, Black, Lower Senior). Many have come to see college degrees as an escape from their communities, and the likelihood of returning is slim to none.

The intellectual or dominant elite, such as business schools and other "professional" schools, and the criteria for success, instills in the minds of many students that fields such as Black Studies are frivolous—that they are simply where Black students go when they want to "relax," "be Black/themselves," and limit their production. Many of these same students are failing to make connections between their "professional training" at school and their communities they leave behind. Thus, incorporating such a content and connection to Black communities has to be done over a period of time: it must be a running stream in all Black Studies courses. This cannot succeed in a stand-alone course.

Third, preparation by Black Studies instructors in arming students with the knowledge to consider the social factors that affect Black people in America is crucial, particularly since the number of Black students attending college is always in a state of flux. The demand of the student activists at SFSU in 1968 was for Black students to be admitted to the school and for the school to establish a Black Studies department to address not only the needs of the Black students but also to enable the connection between student and community. To extract courses and limit course offerings to students in Black Studies is to signal the disconnect between student and community and to set a tone that Black Studies is otherwise not important to the central function of the school.

Fourth, identifying issues and problems faced by Black students and Black community members is another crucial factor in the role of Black Studies. This is even more fundamental if Black Studies is anything but a major area of study at any school. Without teaching and exposing students to the tools necessary and available (as in purposes 1 and 2 above) to them in order to identify such issues, how can they then understand that their role is to provide leadership, to offer a collective to other students as well as community members, to help in resolving these issues, or at least offer a critical attempt at such resolution? The fourth purpose truly highlights the limitations of Black Studies as a minor or certificate, showing the disconnect, dismissal, and potential breakdown of Black Studies' historical and political place at the university.

Using these four major purposes for the overall existence of Black Studies requires the creation of a curriculum that teaches the history of how Black Studies came to be a central focus of the demands of student and community members fighting for equality. To placate students by offering them random courses that may or may not resemble the articulation of difference and struggle, is to deplete their intellectual wealth. During the San Francisco State Strike and what is largely known as the "Birth of Black Studies," purposes for Black Studies departments not only had clear, concise rationales that were connected back to the Black community (outside school) but also had major impacts in Black cultural history. For example, members of the Black Nationalist component of the National Student's Association called for the engagement with and creation of projects based on Black life (both hermeneutically and ontologically). During this movement, Black Nationalist members of the National Student's Association worked to produce *Black Dialogue* (a leading Black Arts magazine) and the *Journal of Black Poetry*.[17] It was the student activists that not only built the Black Studies department at SFSU but also used their scholarship and intellectual activism to help demand as much and more for their fellow community members and classmates. The connection between academics and community was very clear during this movement—this is something that has not been effectively replicated since. The projects, protests, and connections between the two groups are what keep Black Studies surviving in institutions that may or may not value its existence. These same partnerships are what inform students not only of the importance of Black Studies, but its connection to their lives outside of school: their communities, their family structures, and workforce. The partnerships help build positive relationships between people from socially and physically diverse backgrounds. Black Studies "can provide a framework for correcting the misinterpretation and subordination of the African Diaspora" (Norment, 2007, xxxvi) and thus create a coalition of both social and intellectual relations among a diverse student population.

Schools that offer poorly structured programs in Black Studies, and minors rather than majors in the field, fail to discover the connection between Black Studies, their overall student population, intellectual training, and the building of an intellectual identity outside of school and post-graduation. Many critics have long suggested that Black Studies is an intellectually inferior and trivial focus of study that dwells on Black Nationalism and the training of the resistance of students, with no real academic quality or intellectual endurance.

> It [Black Studies] has been stifled in some universities and given a bad reputation by commentators who do not support Black studies or a particular school of thought within the field. Yet, to state that there is no methodology or body of knowledge that grounds the discipline is manifestly erroneous (Christian, 2007, 353).

This attitude of such ill-informed critics supports the notion that American and European historical analysis can include racially oppressed populations in inconsequential mentions, as opposed to extracting this population from the status-quo discourse in traditional courses (History, Sociology, etc.) and examining it in depth. Harold Cruse argued, "Black Studies [is] an instrument of cultural nationalism specifically concerned with critiquing the integrationist ethic and providing a counter-balance to the dominant Anglo-Saxon culture."[18]

While many have argued that instructors of courses in Black Studies should be drawn from "traditional" disciplines in order to strengthen the perspective and presence of the field, I argue that faculty of Black Studies should be housed within Black Studies and should be armed with training in the field or at least be of the organic intellectual camp in which ontological and hermeneutical analyses can be considered as an accurate pedagogical tool. Martin Kilson suggests,

> Black Studies would be more desirable intellectually and academically if scholars who taught in Black Studies were represented in the established departments like classics, philosophy, history and economics and if university facilities adopted the policy of joint academic appointments.[19]

While the basic premise of this suggestion is well received, and is structurally sharp, it also must consider that universities could use this very suggestion to do away with a stand-alone Black Studies department by drawing classes out of existing departments, particularly ones that are traditional and never under threat of loss of institutional funding or low student enrollment. With Kilson's framework, the potpourri of faculty members does not introduce students to a house of Black Studies but only exposes them through windows into specific topics. For this to be successful, funding cannot be an issue, student enrollment must be at a competitive height each semester, and Black Studies must offer a major. Implementation of the potpourri of faculty members resembles the above illustration of random topics in Black Studies, following no stream and having no clear academic outcomes or learning goals. Such a program does not work in congress with the overall university's learning goals for the student body.

> If there is 'failure,' it is often with the universities who do not adequately fund the departments and programs; who do not recruit new faculty when lines become available due to retirement or transfers to other universities; who do not allow for growth and development for Black Studies. Yet, regardless of this, it would still be fallacious to state that the discipline has failed (Christian, 2007, 353).

Faculty with training in the field of Black Studies must be recruited, and they must be able to train students in the same tradition. Through this unified front, methodologies in Black Studies will be examined, but new ones also will be developed through the combination of students and faculty members who work solely on this subject from a variety of perspectives, inculcating the community at every turn.

Joint and affiliated faculty members in Black Studies are extremely important in the overall arc and muscle in sustaining Black Studies at any university, but members of the faculty that are recruited for teaching loads in these programs must exemplify and illustrate their commitment by:

1. The work they produce with their students who enroll in Black Studies as a major or minor.
2. Their relationship to the community, which can be direct and/or benefit from the training of students in Black Studies.
3. Teach equal amounts of courses in Black Studies and their home departments as opposed to simple cross-listing and cross registration.
4. Offer substantial contributions to the curriculum of Black Studies.
5. Present opportunities for students to develop imperative skill sets through Black Studies and the faculty member's home department/training, which will enable them to be competitive in the job market and their communities.
6. Actively recruit Black students and other interested students (preferably from their home departments) to take courses and develop projects for the department of Black Studies.
7. Develop major initiatives through their home departments but jointly with Black Studies, where students can be actively involved.
8. Work collectively with Black Studies-housed faculty members to develop programming, curricula, projects, and publications in the field.
9. Teach a variety of courses that follow through with the mission of the Black Studies Department and are respectful of the historical traditions of Black Studies—which is beneficial to the students in the department and the overall student body as well as the community it serves.
10. Actively represents Black Studies in their home departments by including course offerings and information sessions through their home department functions and events.

The academic responsibilities of those faculty members who are based in Black Studies, as opposed to jointly appointed or departmentally affiliated in other ways, are even more crucial to the representation of the field. A demand of the student activists at SFSU was that the department of Black Studies "grant a Bachelor's Degree in Black Studies; there be a Black Studies department Chair, and faculty and staff have the sole power to hire and fire" for Black Studies. Much should remain true for Black Studies departments today. By allowing the majority of the department to come from other departments, universities may begin to see strength without the Black Studies house. Students who are pursuing graduate degrees in Black

Studies all across the country must be aggressively recruited for teaching in these stand-alone departments. They bring not only historical and traditional training but also contemporary versions of Black Studies that speak to a current generation of learners. Home-based faculty members must:

1. Actively pursue relationships with community members and community-based organizations. These relationships should be pursued where clear links between faculty, community, and Black Studies students can effect change through their intellectual achievement and advancement but also where students are able to and encouraged to explore the world beyond their classroom and engage in political change and community-needed programs.
2. Create service-learning opportunities where faculty and student are inculcated into the lived experience and everyday life of persons not in only school but in the community at large.
3. Continuously publish in journals, online resources, and with a diverse set of publishers, the happenings within their critical academic work in Black Studies.
4. Defend and support junior faculty members; help them to grow in this field by actively encouraging them to work towards tenure; lead by example and standard.
5. Co-publish with students and members of the community on collaborative works produced through such service-learning experiences.
6. Establish relationships with other populations of oppressed groups both in their home countries (on campus and through community organizations) and abroad. Include students and community members in the development of such programming.
7. Aggressively seek institutional and government funding for projects that include further examination of the Diaspora, its culture, and economic development structures. Create funded projects for the university at large to examine as part of the production of knowledge for Black Studies students.
8. Organize and host Black Studies intellectually-based events.
9. Represent the department at major institutional and university committees, such as curriculum, university senates, planning and budget committees, and advisory councils.
10. Represent and advise Black Studies students throughout their academic journey at the undergraduate and graduate levels and mentor them to graduation.
11. Present opportunities for students to work in the department and with individual faculty members to contribute to the growth of their intellectual capacities, as well as the growth of the department.

12. Actively examine the work of all faculty members housed in the department so that resources are clearly exchanged and fairly administered, thus contributing to the overall and collective growth of a united front. These same resources can be used to create initiatives for Black Studies students.
13. Eliminate competition within and among the department's members. Create opportunities within the department for all members of the faculty to contribute to, and seek university-wide initiatives that will help support the work of Black Studies scholars.

These 13 responsibilities are just entryway suggestions for a successful program. As many have written in the past, community-building in Black Studies is as important as intellectual advancement in scholarly productions of knowledge. The corporate construction of many colleges has since been steadfast in pulling students from a world-view opposed to individualistic, hegemonic, and capitalist beliefs in bootstrap ideological practices.

> Corporatized Black leaders who are not directly employed by corporations, are 'sold' to Blacks like toothpaste; they get rich promoting American capitalism while conjuring up the spirits of Martin Luther King in revised corporate minds, while King's anti-capitalist message, and solidarity with the poor is lost. The bling-bling corporatized value system is creating a deranged mindset, while it turns children into obese diabetic consumers of hamburgers, which symbolizes the corporations' desire to create a standardized destiny and non-nutritional diet of imitation, crass consumerism, violence, and depressed spiritual emptiness (SFSU, Africana Studies Department History).

Without the demand for Black Studies as a major, political attacks on the field push us back to the pre-1960s academic struggle for inclusion. Without such a presence, the students make no connection to their lived experience in their role as a native informant to the community. Furthermore, they fail to develop their expertise and begin to lose interest in their history and social positions in our world. A prime example of this arose during one of my Black Studies classes, where we had a general dialogue about the nature of Black communities in New York (where most of them live). The students in my courses, as well as workshop students from other schools, were invited to attend.

Many students commented on the neglect of their communities by city agencies such as Sanitation, the Health Department, Environmental Protection, and the lack of access to basic necessities such as good supermarkets, green groceries, sidewalk garbage cans, adequate lighting of their street, vermin control, trees, traffic lights, and other societal neglect. Yet, the majority of them had become complacent about their living situation, seeing no opportunity to make change and demanding a standard of good living. They either believed they could not make change given their limited time between "work and school" (and for many, "work" also included responsibilities in their homes), and others felt there was no support for such a fight ("what can I do?" was a reoccurring question). The students did not believe collectivism would work. They did not believe their community would rise for change, nor would members of the community be interested. None of them tried for fear of a fighting what they called "a losing battle" and "wastes of time." In addition, many were fearful of the possibility of standing alone in a fight that requires many. They believed that the time of political protest had died with Malcolm X. Without a leader, so vital to any successful movement, change would remain a historical fantasy that was reflected upon but not enacted.

It is my argument that Black Studies could be the vehicle to train these very students on what can be done to make change in these types of communities. It is within the walls of Black Studies, with its rich history of protest and demand, that we can arm these students with the voice and voracity to present themselves as a united front. The leader among them will emerge. For many of them, examples of social change and protest came from history books, classroom lectures, and films; they had not seen this in their reality, nor did their school grounds train them to attempt such an endeavor.[20] Their own belief in their leadership skills is lost to them and to society at large.

Diversity of Social Change Efforts

The students went on to discuss their role as social change agents by hosting and participating at fundraising events for global issues such as the Haitian Relief, the Japanese Earthquake of 2011, the Tsunami of 2004, UNICEF, Red Cross, Cancer awareness (which raised $47,000 one year at one particular school) and AIDS awareness, Backpacks for NYC Kids, and the answering of "Dear Santa" letters. They also worked to raise money for terminal illness walks and runs. Among this particular group of over 100 students (the analysis group for this project), there were previous events hosted around Black Studies, Black communities, or any such related topic, but none since 2006. Many of the students who participated in the school's partnership with Habitat for Humanity's rebuilding of New Orleans in the wake of Hurricane Katrina were not Black. In reaction to this outcome and lack of participation, I designed several projects where students' learning experiences were not only political but required of them—active participation in community building, learning, membership, and advocacy. While some students rejected the work with communities because of "time constraints" and "personal issues," many of them thoroughly enjoyed the building of relationships with the organizations, the community residents, and their children. They were surprised to learn that community partnerships were a tradition among many Black students/scholars. Among the projects created out of several Black Studies courses I taught and later used with the analysis group were:

1. Mobile Literacy Program (MLP). MLP was created in partnership with public schools and after-school organizations in New York City that had high numbers of Black and Latino/a children. The schools and after-school organizations were selected based on racial enrollment (as mentioned) and literacy test scores. After six months working with this population, my own students, while quite excited, made it clear that they were ill equipped to support the many needs of the participating children. One interesting result of their experience came from an Black female student who reported to me that a site counselor (also Black female) shared with her that:

> the children at the after school organization love the lawyers that volunteer with the kids, but they don't like you guys (my students) and your "reading workshops" (Shalice, Black, Sophomore)

Through a bit of research and field notes, the student and I learned that the majority of the lawyers were White and dressed like "business people" (as described by one of the children). In the eyes of these young Black and Latino/a children, success was measured by the appearance of business attire and Whiteness. It was not very often that these children were exposed to educated and academically superior Black folk, neither in their classrooms nor at their after-school organization. In many ways this resembled the attitudes of some of my own students, and those used at the research site's workshop, who had indicated Black Studies wasn't a field they had a desire to pursue full-time—because there are "no jobs with that kind of degree" (Alan, Black, Freshman).

The after-school organization questioned me and my students' interest in them. They repeatedly asked what I wanted in return, and suggested that their "higher ups" would want to know what I wanted in exchange. Without this information, the organization could not commit to a permanent relationship with students or with me. We guaranteed them that our literacy workshops were based out of Black Studies training at the college level, and we wanted to inspire their participating children to read, write, and learn more about themselves and their community. We received no additional help after this declaration, but they allowed us to continue with our workshops for two semesters. The children were the most resistant.

2. Book Drive: I instituted a year-long book drive, where students were allowed to collect and/or donate whatever book they had, found, received, or simply did not want. The books could be brand new, used, or in semi-good condition. We received about 100 book donations from within the group of students participating; one Black Studies faculty member donated three copies of his own book, and Sociology professor donated two suitcases of books. However, many of the students held on to their books, hoping to resell them at the end of the semester. Some declared, "these books are too expensive to donate, and I didn't even read it." (Sheila, Latina, Senior).
3. The Soup Kitchen, Food Pantries & Food Banks: I introduced the soup kitchen option to my own students several times over the course of one semester, but the entire class could not commit to one day of service together. Only individual students on random days were available. By the tail end of the semester, we did collectively organize a meal for 50 homeless men in New York City through a partnership with St. Paul's House in Hell's Kitchen. Many of the students who worked the soup kitchen shift invited their own friends and later other participants from the research site's workshop sessions to serve alongside them.

These are just minor examples of projects that were created for my students, and for students at the research site, for two important reasons: (1) to test collective ideology among Black Studies students, and (2) to implement service learning components into the class. However, without departmental support and university-wide administrative sustaining, the projects were simply a continuation of the conversations on illiteracy, poverty, economic injustice, and hunger that occur throughout the core courses in Black Studies. The students through dialogue alone would fail to see a larger connection to their academic goals unless actively engaging in these projects and projects similar to these that require leaving the classroom. To their credit, many were interested and even inspired that there was such an opportunity presented to them where previously they had none, but the time constraints of their academic lives and the disconnect between learning and community presented difficulty in trying to reintroduce them to the passion of another era.

CHAPTER FOUR

The Black Outcast in the Classroom

Street Lit and Black Academics

The *culture of poverty* (Lewis, 1966)[1] has always had a particular racial undertone to its theoretical presentation. When developed by anthropologist Oscar Lewis in the 1960s, he did not consider the slums, crime, and impoverished climate of White urban dwellers of New York circa 1893. He found no interest in studying these "slum dwellers" (as he identifies Puerto Ricans in *La Vida*[2]), although it was this very population that resulted in the composition of "street literature" and/or "broadside ballads," as they were called between the 16th and 19th centuries. The writings from that time period depict richly descriptive stories and narratives of "street life" that were as gruesome and grizzly as street lit writings of today. The impoverished White British, Irish, and American characters of these broadside ballads are now replaced with Black characters amidst rampant underworld practices.

In Stephen Crane's *Maggie: A Girl of the Streets*, originally self-published in 1893,[3] the depiction of "street life," only populated by poor Whites, gave a clear description of what would become "street lit." Crane's description of a New York slum presented the gritty underbelly of poverty and its residents. Crane wrote about infants and toddlers who found playgrounds in gutters and alley-ways, undergarments hanging on fire escapes waving in the stale air like family flags, litter-lined streets and sidewalks, and women who screamed and cursed among and at each other. He gave readers women who gossiped, beat their children and their husbands while rewarding themselves with over-indulgence of alcohol and domestic violence. However, writings like Crane's *Maggie* did not become catalogued among the examples of early "street literature" or stories that examined the "dark side" of urban dwelling.

Lewis's targets were the Puerto Ricans and Nuyoricans he deemed "slum dwellers," who created their own impoverished situations (both on the island and on the mainland) due to their "low-class" mentality and mirrored behavioral practices. In his ethnographic work, Lewis, like many other social scientists, asked his subjects to expose personal narratives so that the general and/or academic public could get a better understanding of the way "these people" lived life. Today his work is classified as "classic ethnography," used in a variety of sociology classes. The poor, downtrodden, and of-color (in his research) are understood as a bit more human and can be read about in a revered book without actually being encountered on the street.

Black (Street) Life

Street lit has taken on various definitions. It was first popularized in Crane's case with *Maggie: A Girl of the Streets* and later took on a racial, political, and social presentation. A basic definition of the genre is the narrative of those who experience life outside of the margin, a product of poverty, political, and social disenfranchisement. It is important to note that, stereotypically, the "street lit" genre has come to be associated with Blacks at large, when in reality there are Latino/a authors who publish just as frequently as Black writers. It is also important to consider that in urban environments, the underbelly of poverty has no one strand of race, although one race may outnumber other groups in particular communities.

It has also been said that through the writings of street lit novels, Black urbanites can make a connection between their individual lived experience and that of their own racialized group. As a result of such a connection, literacy among this population is said to have increased. A major argument aligned with making connections between lived experience and street lit books is that the books are works of fiction, yet their material bears striking resemblances to "real Black urban ghettos," where characters in these books are not just works of fiction but a reinvention of "the hood."

After the Harlem Renaissance, the narrative of "Black life" took a pause. Thus, the birth, marketing, promotion, sale, and popularity of a new literary genre known variously as street lit, urban fiction, ghetto literature, and now (more commonly) hip hop literature, emerged in the late 1960s. The books had a primary goal of depicting Black "street life" as dangerous, polluted, and in complete opposition to the experiences of the Black literati of the 1920s and 1930s. These novels were not written by the Black high-brows of the Harlem Renaissance and stood in stark contrast to the scholarly presentation of Black identity by W. E. B. Du Bois and Booker T. Washington. Their aim, differing from Du Bois and Washington, was not to write in a way that would necessarily uplift the race but rather it would reproduce clear and realistic examples of Black life on the other side of uplift—the "ghetto." These writings offered Black life as experienced by pimps, ex-convicts, prisoners, and drug fiends-turned-chroniclers. Writers like Donald Goines and Iceberg Slim depicted Black urban communities in all of their oppression, with no attempt to use scholarly language, be accepted into traditional intellectual circles. The writings were responding directly to marginalized communities who were left without a voice and without a choice as to how they were portrayed.

Yet while contemporary street literature acts to resist the myth of the "Happy Negro," writers like Langston Hughes, Wallace Thurman, and Zora Neale Hurston were also resisting dominant elitism among Black and White writers alike. This representation of Black life through literature is not a new concept or recent practice. The context, however, of Black life as written about in both genres remain ostensibly different and something that was feared by many Harlem Renaissance writers—particularly with the multiracial audience that could perhaps use the material as judgment rather than illustration of intellectual achievement. Of Wallace Thurman, Langston Hughes wrote,

> About the future of Negro literature Thurman was very pessimistic. He thought the Negro vogue had made us all too conscious of ourselves, had flattered and spoiled us, and had provided too many easy opportunities for some of us to drink gin and more gin, on which he thought we would always be drunk.[4]

Pimp & Prison Narratives

After emerging from prison, where he had spent much of his days chronicling street life vignettes, Robert Beck, more famously known as "Iceberg Slim," wrote a total of seven books on "Black street life." Beck was noted as one of the first Black writers of street lit. He went on to sell over six million copies of his titles, which were translated into French, Spanish, Italian, Dutch, Swedish, and Greek.[5] It has been written that Beck's White wife, Betty, was the motivation behind his writing career. She explained to Beck that most White people of their time had not been privy to the experiences of Black people like him—her pimp lover—and would find such experiences interesting if they knew of it. To satisfy this type of curiosity, the solution was to shape his lived experience, and the ones Betty was constantly being exposed to, into a book.[6] Slim's versions of street life was always being compared and contrasted to what liberal Whites and Black traditional intellectuals were *not* writing about.

Du Bois constantly urged Blacks to re-educate themselves by continuing to strengthen literacy skills and habits. His ideals worked for a large number of Black scholars, who used the tools he left behind not only to empower themselves but to return to educate their communities. However, some would not apply his very promotion today. As with most ideological practices, or theory to put into practice, Du Bois' sense of urgency for an entire people has become streamlined and directed as having a specific outcome. The re-education did not remain inclusive of all types of knowledge production and consumption.[7] It is inaccurate to believe that new epistemological approaches to writing about Black life would not emerge after such a long haul promoting the examination of the self and later the exploration of that very self, resulting in the re-education of a people. Black street literature, particularly the works of Iceberg Slim and later Donald Goines (both deemed "fathers of urban fiction") was being produced to promote literacy by offering another type of narrative: the organic intellectual voice. A new version of street life, while painful to experience and even recount, became popular, exciting, sociopolitical, and empowering for many to read and write about.

Iceberg Slim was no member of Du Bois's "talented tenth." He was a convicted pimp, con artist, and street hustler who lived as a predator of women with low self-esteem—women who, like him, had succumbed to poverty in unimaginable ways. Betty revealed in an interview that Slim did not believe composition of his life in book format would save their family from poverty.[8] Beyond the margins of mainstream society, Slim did not see the importance of his life prior, during, and after his bout with street life. Here, the complexity of White patronage, Black scholarship, and the question of who produces and consumes Black thought, becomes central. How the texts are used in Black Studies, and who is teaching these texts, becomes part of the discussion among Black Studies scholars and students alike.

After composing several narratives, the Becks answered an ad in the newspaper that shouted "Black writers needed! Publisher will pay you for your stories."[9] It was clear, however, that the publishers were not looking for Harlem Renaissance writers. They were looking for alternatives to Black scholarly outlooks on life. The publisher was seeking the narrative of the underdog. Bentley Morris, white CEO of Holloway House Publishers, was clear that he did not want to read about Blacks and their "trips abroad."[10] Instead, Morris wanted to read about the Black experience written by members within the Black community as opposed to researchers studying the community from outside. Morris saw real narratives of Black life in Beck's writing. Beck's pimping-, drug-, and crime-ridden experiences instantly impressed Morris. Morris and his editors felt the reality within Beck's writing. His "street style" included the use of endless profanity and an abundance of slang, along with vulgarity and sexually explicit vignettes. Morris was not alone in his admiration of Beck's work. Many in the Black community reported that they had not been able to connect and/or identify with the literature of the Harlem Renaissance or the Civil Rights movement. The generation that Beck represented had missed both the Harlem Renaissance and Civil Rights movement, and although many were fully immersed in a version of Black power ideological beliefs and practices, the traditional sense of such a practice seemed buried somewhere. Therefore, it has been argued that this emerging genre spoke to a larger population of displaced and disconnected Black readers while replacing the traditional intellectual writings of this racial group within a mainstream audience.

From Hustler to Prisoner to Chronicler

Employing a critical and analytical lens, we can examine the two major figures in street lit (Beck and Goines). Their most important novels, *The Naked Soul of Iceberg Slim*[11] and *Dopefiend*,[12] were introductions to the complexities of "Black street life." Picking up in a part of society that the Harlem Renaissance could not reach, street literature begins to unpack questions about the authenticity of such narratives and the interpretation of Black lived experience.

Donald Goines, like Robert Beck, published several novels that gained notoriety among Black readers. Together, their books assisted in popularizing a new genre of literature for Black writers from urban backgrounds. Among some of Goines's more famous titles were *Whoreson*[13] and *White Man's Justice, Black Man's Grief*.[14] All of his writings created a narrative of street life that included gruesome examples of the production and consumption of poverty. Goines narrates the victimization of ghetto residents as well as the self-victimization caused by concentrated acts of global and internal oppression.

Much of the authenticity of Goines's work came from his own life experience, in which he was a junkie, pimp, and blue-collar worker, along with a career as a hard-core criminal. A question about his authenticity does arise, however, when considering that his life did not begin in poverty nor in a slum, unlike his predecessor Iceberg Slim. Goines was a child during the Detroit race riot in 1941, but his family remained untouched by the incident. His father's dry cleaning business was also unharmed by the riots. Goines's father owned and operated the business along with his wife, and Donald later became an employee there.[15]

Goines dropped out of school by the 9th grade, finding more affection for sports and hustling than he did in any classroom.[16] By the time he was 24, he was a dope-fiend and a pimp who was learning the rules of the dark side of life. Like many street-lit writers (both historical and contemporary writers), Goines found more offerings in the underground world than he did working a legitimate blue-collar job.

> He entered the pimping profession with serious intent. To hell with a job. He had always been best suited for self-employment, anyway. So why not make a living on his own terms (56).

In many ways, the writing style of his literary hero, Robert Beck, allowed him to develop a voice to compose his own version of life in the "Black ghetto." Although the narratives of Beck and Goines exhibit small differences, and they themselves differ in terms of skin color (one darker than the other, which is significant among prostitutes as well as with pimp stature), the overall street life experiences parallel one another. Both writers depicted the grisliest of slum experiences. Beck's *The Naked Soul of Iceberg Slim* opens with:

> In the cold-blooded academy of ghetto streets I was taught early that suffering is inevitable and necessary for an aspiring pimp, pickpocket or con man and even just a nigger compelled to become a four-way whore for the Establishment (Beck, 1971, 17).

Although all of Beck's and Goines's books fit neatly into the street-lit genre, all of them also had a streak of activism that attempted to showcase the lived experience of Blacks, the downtrodden, and perhaps the government who had forgotten about this population. The theory of ghettoization is employed here to explain the emergence and popularity of the genre due to the social realities of the Black experience during the 1960s and the 1970s. The voice and experience of the Black and politically disenfranchised needed an outlet. The experience, however, would be told by way of shocking imagery with even more shocking narration. For many Black young males from the "inner cities" of America, their communities offered, and in many instances still do offer, minimal opportunities to gain legitimate living-wage employment. The pimp narrative presented itself as an alternative for these men who, at one time, had sought legal employment. The transformation from unemployed and downtrodden to recognized pimp for many, was the ultimate achievement of power in the ghetto. "To these men in power [pimps], it is a game in which they control and manipulate the actions of others subordinate to them."[17] This definition can also be understood and applied to the construction of the cyclicality of oppression and its dependents—the oppressor and the oppressed and their reversals of (mis)fortune.[18]

It can be argued that Goines and Beck were presenting a "global" experience shared by large numbers of Black impoverished members of society. Alongside Beck and Goines writing pimp and junkie narratives, Black poets like Amiri Baraka were composing revolutionary pieces, and Malcolm X could be found recording his monumental speeches. A key point here is that while all of these authors were writing about life experiences, Beck and Goines inspired convicts and ex-felons not only to begin their writing careers in prison but upon release from prison, to open up their own publishing houses which focused on street literature.

Attempting to escape from White patronage (such as Beck's dealings with Bentley Morris) or frustrated from having White editors reject their work or twist the narrative into something of an imitation of Black composition, many contemporary street-lit writers are now either self-published or are publishing their work through Black-owned street-lit presses. The question remains, as it did during the writing days of both Beck and Goines, are these narratives and their authors adequate, universal, authentic representations of "Black urban culture,"[19] and where and how can educators begin to reinsert these narratives into the college classroom? The evolution and popularity of the genre became and still remain two-fold. Firstly, this genre represents a voice less discovered and nearly invisible in the college classroom, and secondly, it promotes the production of a new knowledge that has resulted in improved literacy among reluctant Black readers. Ultimately, to exclude this genre from academic discussion, particularly in a Black Studies class, is to completely eliminate an entire genre of writing, a population of readers/writers, and a particular voice from the conversation. Eliminating the work from such a Black Studies class is also to adopt the attitude that alienated people like Goines and Beck from mainstream classrooms.

Narrations on Oppression

Within the oppression and prison narrative (which makes up a huge part of street-lit novels), two important elements within the works of both Beck and Goines are the objectification/exploitation of Black women and the development of a hyperviolent Black masculinity. Central to the writings of Beck and Goines, as well as more current authors, is the exhibition of the revered "heroic hustler."[20] This exalted neighborhood and genre hero was the ideal response to the disconnection from "real" Black role models dwelling in Black American ghettos. This street lit hustler is a learned man from the street, whose qualities include vulgarity and degradation. Yet his brute force, his "way with the ladies," and his maneuvering on the streets allow him to keep his "heroic hustler" status. The Black pimp and/or hustler has more fans and mentees than he knows what to do with. Iceberg Slim was receiving letters from young Black men who addressed him as their "mentor," testifying their hopes at becoming just like him. Additionally, Black fathers were giving copies of Iceberg Slim's books to their young sons.[21] The Black pimp book had become a manifesto/guide for Black men dwelling in urban ghettos. Yet this figure, while present in important places such as letter-writing and father–son exchanges, was not being discussed in classrooms—one of the most important places to decontextualize the oppression of the heroic hustler. *Pimp*, by Slim is later noted:

> The book emerges as a kind of fusion of school textbook (for young men disaffected with, disappointed by, and economically excluded from institutionalized schooling), a sacred players' bible, and a self-help or etiquette manual on sexual relations and style practices, all of which involve very active reading practices (Quinn, 2001, 220).

While the pimp as "heroic hustler" is celebrated in many ways in particular literature and music for being a "consummate capitalist," he is also revered as a pedagogue that broke Black male slave stereotypes of being lazy, brawn over brain, having "sexual wantonness and sexual prowess."[22] Yet, he is invisible in collegiate culture and collegiate dialogue.

> Nowadays in the imperialist white-supremacist capitalist patriarch culture, most boys from poor and under-privileged classes are socialized via mass media and class-biased education to believe that all that is required for their survival is the ability to do physical labor. Black boys, disproportionately numbered among the poor, have been socialized to believe that physical strength and stamina are all that really matter (hooks, 2004, 39).

While excluded from academic discourse, this heroic hustler grows stronger in his underground narrative and attracts more young men (and women) than figures in plain sight. This invisibility not only continues to perpetuate his oppression but also continues to marginalize populations that do not see themselves represented in academic structures.

In many of these "pimp narratives," Black and White women alike are physically, sexually, verbally, and emotionally abused all in one setting, and at incredible levels. Although many of the female characters in the works of Goines, Beck, and newer street literature authors alike, are sassy, verbally abusive (to one another and to men), loveless, and have some type of independence (as defined by "the hood,") they are intimidated by Black males, particularly one that is characterized as a "pimp." In historical reflection of a Black woman's obloquy at the hands of her White slave owner and/or her White mistress, in street lit, her persecutor is her Black male counterpart. It can be inferred here then that street lit is not only a narrative of the oppressed but of the oppressor as well.

When historical Black writing discussed social injustices, whether in the format of fiction, nonfiction, memoir, and/or poetry (Black Arts Movement), the tone always seemed outwardly sociopolitical. Street lit, however, depicts racism as the means to an end. For example, Donald Goines, as previously mentioned, did not grow up impoverished and was more victimized by his own circle for being light-skinned than he was by Whites for being Black (Allen, 2004). It can be argued, then, that this genre began as the Black male version of sociopolitical writing, indirectly responding to the social injustices they faced within their own communities. It can also be argued, however, that many of the "heroic hustlers" and "gutter Gods"[23] were responding to psycho-social and/or social emotional issues to life in their own households. This is a very accurate analysis of some authors. In *The Naked Soul of Iceberg Slim*, Beck suggests that while in prison, a psychiatrist discussed with him the possibility that he may have gone towards pimping because of his difficult relationship with his mother.

> Looking back, I remember that the most efficient and brutal pimps I have known had mothers who were drunkards, dope fiends, or whores. Several of the cruelest pimps that come to mind were abandoned as infants. One was put in a trash bin and another was stuffed into a garbage can. I am positive that as much as anything else my boyhood admiration for the flash and dazzle of well-heeled pimps cruising the poverty-mauled slums in gaudy cars inspired me to pimp (Beck, 1971, 58).

Both the old and newer titles in the genre have been called "narrative realities"[24] in that they reflect Black humanity. Daunting is the fact that these "narrative realities," particularly in the majority of the original Black street literature novels, offer no plausible solution to the plight and sociopolitical struggle of being Black, poor, and exposed to some of life's grittiest and grimiest experiences. In humanity there is always a duality, but the duality here is contingent upon the articulation of oppression as cyclical. Thus the oppressed become the oppressors, who continue to oppress each other without any reason or rationale except that they are all members of the underclass, no matter what little "power" they have. Again, this is revisited in college classrooms that do not present these narratives among their required readings broadly, but rather confined them to courses on "prison writings" and the overarching "African American literature" courses.

In its early beginnings, Black street literature was and still remains an important member and voice of the Black literary canon. The entire genre juxtaposed the life of those traditionally trained in schoolhouses to those with organic experiences and expertise. Having taken on several different identifications in bookstores, among readers, publishing houses, librarians and the writers themselves, the genre has replaced Black sociopolitical and nonfiction work.

Although many of the street-lit narratives are transformed into scholarly work by intellectuals, and the ideas co-opted by those who argue the same position as the street-lit authors, the genre itself is not widely introduced in classrooms for fear of presenting "non-serious" literature. This creates a tension within many public library acquisitions roundtables, who wish to acquire more street-lit titles due to popular demand of young, as well as older, Black readers.[25] If college courses are not introducing and teaching the genre, the books remain at the request of community members who are not otherwise presented with books that relate to themselves and their life experience. It is arguable however, that without this type of "traditional" training, the books are mass consumed for their face value. While they are relatable to community experiences, they are not being critically discussed with college students—many of whom have come from the backgrounds described in some street-lit titles. The Black underclass still exists. As Black street literature continues to rise in popularity, some 30–40 years after its inception, it offers no real comprehensive interpretation and/or understanding of the Black sociopolitical dilemma and no feasible solutions—at least not collectively. Many of the current titles continue to depict the Black underclass as minimally literate, poorly educated, but eager to enter the underworld happenings of crime and drugs as an escape from poverty. Further exclusion of the books from academic discussion creates a perception that school does not reflect reality and vice versa.

> Anti-intellectualism in black communities is often a weapon used in the class warfare between those black folks who feel condemned to a narrow existence because they are not educated and are therefore unable to be upwardly mobile [...] These privileged-class educated black folks have tended to regard the uneducated with contempt. And the uneducated have responded by reflecting that contempt (hooks, 1994, 43).

If we consider Fisher's (2009) position on reading and literate Black communities,[26] street-lit books offer comprehensive presentation of social ills and conditions. However, they also attempt to gloss particular behaviors as a result of such sociopolitical disenfranchisement. The narrative mantra becomes "this is who we are, this is our narrative, these are our experiences, from prison-to-paper." The paradox of the "Black experience" as told by Black street literature writers, like Beck and Goines, became a marker of authenticity. Many of the current authors attempt to continue in Beck's writing tradition but fall short when it comes to presentation of such an underworld. Bentley Morris, Beck's White publisher, was seen as a predator who profited from the negative narratives of Black (and predominantly male) writers, leaving many of them famous but even more impoverished than before their "literary fame." In an interview with Mark Skillz, Beck's daughter indicated that her father had no traditional intellectual skills or scholarly sass to interpret the terms in his writing contracts with Holloway House and thus was essentially "robbed" by Morris. At the time of his liver failure, and ultimately his death in 1992, Beck was found living in a gang-riddled neighborhood, "in a one-bedroom apartment with barely [any] running water and leaky pipes,"[27] unable to pay for dialysis treatment and not understanding the level of his fame brought on by his work. Perhaps if they taught in academic settings and critically analyzed, his books would have been kept within the current publishing circle and held in higher regard than just sidewalk sales and underground fame.

Street Lit in Various Hands

As discussed in the chapter, "Pimpin' Ain't Easy," Quinn reasserts that pimps were seen as clever capitalists who

> were aspiring magnates of materialism who needed no Wharton School credentialization to understand that organized crime occupied an unhallowed but secure place on the continuum of American business systems.[28]

Yet, both Beck and Goines died in poverty, and in worse circumstances than what originally drove them towards the life. Current personifications of the "Black pimp" are now associated with Hip Hop music and its celebrities.[29] In agreement with Robin Kelley, many Black pimps, through the prostitution industry and sex trade, were engaging in this underground employment option to escape from wage-work, and thus more quickly gain a larger amount of money with which they could access material commodities that their Black blue-collared working counterparts lacked.

One argument as to why street literature is not included in college classrooms is that it is quite limiting in its ideas, use of language, and visual (book covers) presentations. Second, while many support the argument that these books create a higher rate of literacy among young, Black, reluctant and "at risk" readers, it is not being used to engage populations that are already literate. As a form of new Black epistemology, street literature can be defined as a community narrative that is assumed as being widely experienced by Black people as well as other groups living in the same circumstances. Considering historical Black epistemology and its current position, street literature writers who begin their craft in prison create Black thought as a complex experience to summarize. However, these experiences are important to the analysis of a people and production of knowledge, particularly in a Black Studies classroom where every avenue of Black identity should be investigated. Author Debra J. Dickerson reflects on the writing of Ralph Ellison, whom she identifies as a member of the Black bourgeoisie,[30] as having two parts to what she considers "racial fraud syndrome." She writes,

> On one level they merely lack civic confidence, but on another they are civic terrorists actively at war with America and fighting for their psychological life. For without their oppression they are no one special, run-of-the mill Americans, bores until proven otherwise. And they alone are responsible for their own betterment and their own problems, with the resources of a largely benevolent nation behind them. They are average Joes with average lives to lead. Theirs is neither the victim's nor the hero's glamour (Dickerson, 2004, 11).

When Black writer Nick Chiles critiques street literature, he accuses the genre of perpetuating an example of Black self-sabotage. About the position of his own books on bookstore shelves, he states,

> we were all represented under African American literature, the whole community of black authors, from me to Terry McMillan and Toni Morrison, surrounded and swallowed whole by an overwhelming wave of titles and jackets that I wouldn't want my 13-year-old son to see (Fialkoff, 2006).

In turn, writer Nikki Turner, who has authored titles like *Natural Born Hustler* (One World/Ballantine, 2010), and *A Hustler's Wife* (Triple Crown Productions, 2003), states,

> I am not interested in how we look to white people. I am interested in literacy in the community and being able to get people to read books who have never read before (Dodson, 2006).

Chiles's position suggests that street-lit books are inappropriate for young adults, and for this reason and perhaps others, he did not support the placing of his books in sections that also housed street-lit titles. Turner's response suggests that where Black literacy is struggling among impoverished communities, there is another urgent call for self–re-education that fights against what the dominant elite believes is quality writing. It is clear that Black epistemology has two different camps, as mentioned throughout this chapter, and that these two camps are each quite aware of their audience. Turner defends her work as reaching out to Blacks who do not engage in reading books without being prompted. While Turner presents an incredibly strong argument, it is also important to note that an even stronger influence would be to include the books in college classrooms, particularly Black Studies classrooms, where the books can begin to be investigated by those studying in the field.

Writing and Analysis for Young Folk

Whereas the writing of the Black (traditional) intellectual was generally reserved for the scholarly reader (who was equipped to interpret and digest such works), street literature as a contemporary form of Black epistemology has become a fan favorite among people of a younger generation. Many arguments have been made in support of street lit being the new genre of literature that helps to entice reluctant young readers of color and thus increases their rates of literacy overall as mentioned earlier. Librarians, in particular Young Adult (YA) librarians, host and attend national conferences on street literature book-clubbing and acquisitions. Hundreds of lists are released and published every year with top titles that "reluctant" readers of color (more specifically Black and Latino/a youth) may be attracted to. It is important to note that neither Goines nor Beck is represented in these current lists or advertisements for young readers of street literature. In just 30–40 years, part of the history is being lost for younger readers, and an improper handling of such information distribution has been activated.

While many current street-lit titles are inspired by real prison experience and related types of narratives, they can be coupled with the prison experience writings of Malcolm X and George Jackson. Many contemporary genre authors have had to withstand the test of "street authenticity" and/or the "code of the street"[31] in order to gain respect among readers. Many college courses that do introduce street lit in their syllabi do so under the heading of "prison writings" or "prison narratives" and or a variation of writings by "the other." While this may present an erroneous grouping of the Black experience as per as Chiles's argument, it does present a less confrontational way at introducing the collective experience of social and political disenfranchisement.

> Although Goines has scant chance of being studied in the future as a literary giant, he could be studied then, and certainly ought to be today, as a gigantic cultural influence (Franklin, 2008, 646).

Here, I will provide an overview of how street lit has been incorporated in some of the college courses that have taken the initiative in including it in their curriculum[32]:

Assigned in one course, titled "Black Pulp Fictions" and among the required books, were *Dopefiend* and *Pimp: The Story of My Life*. The course was offered out of an English department. A second course, titled "20th Century Prison Literature," presented three learning outcomes[33]:

1. An awareness of the breadth, depth, and quality of the writing produced by prison inmates during the 20th century.
2. An acquaintance with the work of some dozen or more writers whose output would be considered significant in any circumstances.
3. A greater compassion for the incarcerated with an admiration for their accomplishments in adversity.

Assigned in this course was a session dedicated to "Civil Rights Movement in Prison" and listed there was *The Autobiography of Malcolm X*, *Letter from Birmingham Jail*, *Soledad Brother*, excerpts from *Soul on Ice* by Eldridge Cleaver, and *Naked Soul* by Iceberg Slim. It seems here that "quality" as used in outcome number 1 and learning to grow a "greater compassion for the incarcerated" (as per learning outcome number 3) leave the reader of the required books with an expertise in defining "quality" among writers emerging from prison. In addition, the compassion sought after as a collective outcome removes the societal implications for why these writers wrote such pieces in prison, and perhaps why they even went to prison in the first place. Seeking compassion because they have emerged from prison with a literary ability amidst their having faced such adversity sensationalizes their racial and political places in the literary world. Perhaps through a Black Studies class, "compassion" would be replaced by critical (de)contextualization. While there is a sense of feeling and emotion involved in reading anyone's narrative, those very readers (especially Black Studies students) are trained to analyze the narrative in critical ways that affect the process and progress of our world/society.

A third syllabus, from a course on "American Crime" regards street-lit authors Sister Souljah and Vickie Stringer as contemporary urban authors unlike the comparisons to pioneering Black crime writers like Chester Himes and Iceberg Slim (both also taught in this class).

Syllabi like these offer a direct reflection of the popularity that street lit is gaining among various members in our literate communities. In order to understand the genre better, as opposed to classifying it as "trashy reads," it is a necessity that college classrooms integrate these books into their curricula. When poet Sonia Sanchez was interviewed about her perspective on street lit, she reported,

> I'm delighted even about street literature. I believe we should write everything. Everybody else writes everything; why shouldn't we? When I was growing up, I used to read what we called racy literature. I was at the library every bloody day, and racy literature kept me reading (Moore, 2010).

The inclusion of street literature in college classrooms, particularly in the field of Black Studies, offers a critical and intellectual examination into the genre, as previously mentioned, but also helps to dispel stereotypes surrounding those marginalized by society. In reflection of Sanchez's argument, much can be applied to those who make this argument for other genres. For example, Antonia Losana at Middlebury College argues for the inclusion of popular romance novels (à la Harlequin) that are becoming popular among English literature classes and particularly in her own classes:

> A course just on popular romance runs the risk of isolating and marginalizing the popular romance—as if we were trying to keep it from infecting the *Beowulf* to Virginia Woolf survey, for example. It has been my strategy to include at least one popular romance novel into the syllabus of each course I teach, encouraging students to realize that the boundaries between romance fiction and "canonical" fiction are more permeable than critics of the former would like (Losano, 2011).[34]

In his article, "Can the Penitentiary Teach the Academy How to Read," Professor H. Bruce Franklin reflects on his course "Crime and Punishment in American Literature" in which he hesitantly, but eventually, assigned *Dopefiend*. Franklin remembers that some of the students from that class "were almost all the first generation in their working-class families to attend college and were themselves working, at least part time" (Franklin, 647). Franklin even had police officers, prison guards and ex-convicts in the class. The course prompted a major debate as the definition of "literature," and many of the students took issue with Goines's "limited vocabulary, short sentences, lack of metaphors, and even errors in grammar" (Franklin 647). However, the class discussion, inspired by reading Goines, led to philosophical questions about the definition of literature, and perhaps its representation among the intellectual elite. Important in Franklin's pedagogical moment, and quite specific to the argument being made here, is the revelation by one of his students:

> The first black woman who had spoken up announced, with obviously forced calmness, "my mother gave me my first Donald Goines novel, *Black Girl Lost*, when I was thirteen. That's what made me into a reader. That's what made me love literature. That's why I'm an English major. And that's why I want to be a writer" (Franklin, 648).

Very clearly illustrated in Franklin's student is the example of how powerful street literature is as a pedagogical tool that can be used to inspire and cultivate talents that go untapped by traditional forms of schooling.

Shelving Street Lit at College

Now that it is pushed to a younger reading population, street literature has raised many eyebrows regarding its content. An article written for *The Root* in 2009 suggested that students[35] should "forget about *Paradise Lost* and *The Canterbury Tales*"[36] and pick up any of the 25 books identified in the article's list. Among the well-put-together list was *The Coldest Winter Ever*,[37] one of the major texts in street literature. The above presentation of street literature's introduction into the hands of young Black learners (even the younger college student) begins to consider the presentation of Black epistemology in the college classroom. As you will read in chapter 5 of this book, there is an ever-present question about what Black Studies is not, what it has become, and what it needs to become in its future. One such idea is the exclusion and inclusion of the organic intellectual in such a classroom. Thinking about the ways in which:

> drawing on the black experience induces social studies teachers and other cultural workers to address the Black aesthetic. Such a perspective turns everyday life into aesthetic objects of perception; in such a context, people, lived activities, tragedies, and celebrations can be viewed in a moral, political, and ethical context (Kincheloe, 2001, 641).[38]

For Black students, Black Studies represents a place where there is a shared if not common knowledge among its members. In its contemporary form, Black Studies has begun to include voices from marginalized productions of youth culture, for example, college courses on Hip Hop (Black Studies and Sociology based). Many street literature authors, from Goines to Souljah, have been noted as the forerunners of the genre that inspired Hip Hop lyricism and the depiction of "street life" in music. Thus, it is important to include this voice in these classrooms as well. The breadth of street lit is so wide that to include these works in English classes alone cannot suffice in trying to build an academic understanding of the genre, movement, and culture behind its writings. The offering of college courses on Hip Hop, whether based out of Black Studies or other social studies programs, has seen a rise in registration. The topic resonates with many Black students who clearly identify with the music, the artist, the lyrics, and perhaps even the narrative and lifestyle of the culture. Many Black Studies students (in particular) see the course as an inclusion of a voice that has been extracted from the mainstream college history of "core curricula." While Hip Hop may have been a marker in present-day Black Studies offerings, one can still argue that textual analysis of the literary portion of the culture is still missing from such dialogue. A review of Hip Hop courses and their syllabi is presented here in an attempt to argue that there is cultural space and a necessity to include street-lit titles.

The first syllabus reviewed is for a course on the politics of Hip Hop which explores its history, development, political influence, and standing as well as its social influence.

1. The course is offered from an Ethnic Studies discipline, but it is not clear what specific area of "Ethnic" is targeted. The course requires one book, *That's the Joint! The Hip-Hop Studies Reader*, (Forman and Neal, 2004) and its structural/assignment requirements include: weekly quizzes, song lyric critiques, and performance analysis, as well as a midterm and final exam.[39] The course also requires a listening assignment which is made available at the school library's reserves area. Although the course utilizes most of the readings in the required text and some additional articles (as noted in the syllabus), the course also introduces students quite briefly to the international perspective of Hip Hop.
2. The second syllabus approaches the topic of Hip Hop through the historical journey of this production of culture within its formative years. Hip Hop is presented in this course as a movement based in struggle specifically by Blacks, but also inclusive of Latino/as.[40] The syllabus promises to cover a wide variety of issues such as education, housing, activism, media, film, and literature among its topics. *Yes Yes Y'all: The Experience Music Project Oral History of Hip-hop's First Decade* (Fricke and Ahearn, 2002) and *Taking the Train: How Graffiti Art Became an Urban Crisis in New York City* (Austin, 2001) are required texts, but *The Vibe History of Hip-Hop* (Light, 1999) is recommended as well. The syllabus, however, does not provide the reading schedule.
3. The third course reviewed considers the sociopolitical presentation of Hip Hop and the impact Hip Hop has made on not only productions of culture but also on racial identity.

None of the undergraduate syllabi for Hip Hop courses that were reviewed for this project included street-lit titles or excerpts, nor did they broach the topic within the course's content. The class/syllabus discovered that was in fact solely based on street-lit narratives was a graduate class within a Master's degree program for Urban Studies.[41] The class opened up with a first session on "street literature" (the movement) and connected the genre to the cultural composition of Hip Hop. Included in this course was a session on Black vernacular, social issues (such as the crack epidemic and urban developments), the American prison system, gender and sexuality, and genres of Black writing. The course also included a field trip to Harlem and the Bronx. The course required the following texts:

1. *Teri Woods: True to the Game.* New York: Teri Woods Publishing, 1999.
2. *Donald Goines: Black Gangster.* Los Angeles: Holloway House, reprinted 2006.
3. *Jihad: Street Life.* Deer Park: Urban Books, 2004.
4. *Freeze: Against the Grain.* New York: One World (Random House), 2008 (excerpts).
5. *Thugs and the Women Who Love Them.* New York: Kensington, 2005.

Among the additional readings for this class, there were also selections from various books that deal with Hip Hop cultural productions (including Black vernacular), with a total of seven street-lit titles in their entirety. While the course is only offered to graduate students, these kinds of syllabi can be easily reproduced for the undergraduate Black Studies student, particularly as an introduction to the genre (through the lens of a scholarly investigation) that could potentially lead to a more advanced secondary undergraduate course or a graduate course such as this one.

Serious consideration of the topics offered to the Black Studies student is not only a curriculum issue but also stems from the desire to create well-rounded students in rigorous pursuit of an education. Many undergraduates who have participated in some of the workshops arranged for this project were fans of Hip Hop but rejected street-lit narratives as a qualified form of Black writing, even though it inspired the musical and cultural movement they participate in. This rejection of the genre was based on the extraction of such literature within their school's curriculum requirements and elective offerings. These students could not envision a classroom where these types of books would be taken seriously; thus they believed the entire genre to be of little value, with no contribution to a critical learning experience, not even in Black Studies, where the genre is able to find a comfortable intellectual home. Additionally, none of the titles were available throughout their college library, and they did not see college peers reading the titles on campus. Yet, while the students did not see the genre as valuable to the Black Studies experience, the Hip Hop courses were always full. The invisibility of street lit in the classroom, specifically in Black Studies, where Black students are looking to be exposed to a wholeness of the Black social and political experience, adds to the invisibility of students of Black Studies.

Discussions about these books, while not often found in the classroom, are constantly found on internet forums, which students may or may not frequent. The idea of including street-lit narratives in the Black Studies classroom (and perhaps even in English literature classrooms, as previously discussed) is to dissect the genre with a critical and intellectual eye. It is in these spaces that the educator can assist in promoting the work of the organic intellectual, giving the organic intellectual a voice, and perhaps critiquing the writings in ways that produce a better and more just analysis from readers. Online forum discussions introduced critique of the writings such as: "there is something wrong with the publishing industry for glorifying a lifestyle of sex, drugs, crime and violence, marketing it to blacks and then the black folks running to buy it" (online reader 1, 2006). A response to the above reader claimed that after Terry McMillan's *Waiting to Exhale* was published, an "explosion of sex in the hood" (online reader 2) books was bound to follow. This comment also suggested that street literature was permissible, as long as works of "serious fiction" were also being published at the same rate.

The imbalance in quality and intellectual identity is recognized here in this argument as it has been by various critics of street lit and among the students who participated in the Black Studies workshops. As many Black authors who write "serious fiction" cannot find literary agents to represent them, nor can they get their work published by mainstream houses, there still remains a population that is able to identify their own experiences in street literature. Engaging the Black Studies student in an intellectual discussion about the goals of street literature requires the skill to at least begin to decontextualize these books and consider how they fit into and represent the diverse Black experience(s) in America.

Critical intellectuals, both organic and traditional, can work together to decipher what the books' main goals are. Perhaps the intent is the message of morality (hence why many of the street-lit narratives have moral endings). For example, the third reader on the online forum reflects on her college literature class and comments:

> we [in her class] discussed whether Black authors have an obligation to their race to write positive literature that 'uplifts' the race (online reader 3).

Another question could be to then ask: what constitutes "uplift"? To uplift can mean that college curricula, specifically in Black Studies, can begin to include street literature narratives to represent the Black organic intellectual who writes from his/her street experience and natural environment. Extracting this voice from contemporary or historical conversations about Black literature is to create a simplistic standard for Black literacy, one that does not focus on the self, and one that does not consider the lived experience of those outside and on the margin. Many readers in the online discussion wrote less than desirable comments about various street literature books, while a handful of readers supported the idea that the books, while seemingly "trashy," did help to create a population of readers where otherwise there would not have been one. For those who cannot identify with the traditional intellectual and scholarly works in Black writing but can readily testify to the experience of street life, this genre is critical in understanding the complexity of the Black experience in the United States.

College has a responsibility to expose students to materials, ideas, and practices that encourage discovery. As you have read thus far and will continue to understand, Black Studies serves much larger responsibilities, particularly to its own students. Repetition of information is expected during one's college experience. Introducing street lit (for example) into the curricula (those specifically based in literature) exposes students to a world outside of this very repetition and gives students the ability to truly experience a diverse and less-discovered world.

CHAPTER FIVE

Black Studies Projects
The Communal Class, Samples and Resources

Black Studies as examined in this book, while political in its presence at the university alone, remains in constant flux. This is particularly true when it comes to exhibiting its larger importance to the overall collegiate community, aside from representing Black pedagogy and Black students. Students registering for the courses are not always predominantly Black and/or Latino/a.

To reflect on the earlier chapters and sentiments in this book, it is important to revisit the idea that where Black Studies is not a major area of study, students are subjected to potpourri course offerings where even introductions to the subject need introductions. Students have to begin courses not only with knowledge of key figures and movements in Black Studies but also with the ability to relate to the course material—recognizing that their access to such a program and/or course on the topic should have an impact on their social, personal, and political lives. This is particularly true for Black students, who take courses in Black Studies as a way to socially ground themselves in their intellectual development. Students of Black Studies also need to be involved in projects outside of the classroom texts and discussions that address their needs duality (or their identity-trade) and apply their expertise in topics that are important to them. Community and service-learning integrated courses can help begin to reestablish this historical work in, of, and about Black Studies. For many schools who struggle to keep their Black Studies programs alive, the reality is that students taking these courses need to be involved in the direction of the classes and should be made fully aware of their role as activists in the field and in the larger social world. These programs cannot exist without their social and political efforts and cannot fully thrive in environments where second-class citizenship is not only part of how students are treated but how "minority" programs and scholarship are also treated.

As I have mentioned, for the last 10 years or so I have worked endlessly not only to revamp and reenergize course syllabi for the Black Studies classes that I teach but also to create different projects for the students so that they may apply what they have learned to real-life situations. My communal-class structure is not only feasible but easily accessible to the students and can be adapted by other professors in the field. Based on the historic precedent of Black Studies programs, students in contemporary college classrooms have to be allowed to integrate their lived experience into the classroom—simply reading and writing and relating their narratives will achieve the full objective of Black Studies. In this chapter, I provide key examples of projects I have created for my Black Studies classes as well as books that have helped students identify Black Studies as academically rigorous as any other course.

The goal is to have Black Studies students leave the class at the end of each semester with not only a sense of fellowship with other Black Studies students (something many Black students suggested as the reason for taking Black Studies courses in the first place) but also with a sense of academic achievement and sociopolitical impact/worth. It is imperative that college experiences for students who take Black Studies classes, whether as a major or an elective (but specifically the latter), continue to find a home in these programs to combat the insecurities and isolation they may feel.

Course Projects

As mentioned in the first chapter, introductory courses at universities where Black Studies is a major area of study do an extremely good job of presenting a solid scholarly and social foundation to the discipline. As a major, Black Studies students are generally required to take somewhere between 30 and 35 credits in the field. Having the opportunity to take 10 or 12 classes in Black Studies allows for a traditional introduction to key figures and movements in the field. As a graduate student of the late Dr. Manning Marable, I often reviewed and assisted in the creation of his undergraduate syllabi. His "Introduction to African American Studies" was one of the most comprehensive course creations, I have seen. Although available through the Columbia University website,[1] I will excerpt portions of the syllabus here as well.

Although the course is for undergraduates, there is both a lecture session and a discussion session. Dr. Marable would lead the lecture, where ferocious note-taking would occur. A teaching assistant (usually a graduate student) would lead the discussion session, where important questions about the readings would be raised and discussed. Every student was required to lead at least one discussion during the session by raising key points mentioned in the reading and during the lecture. Students had the option of writing either two formal papers, or one paper and engaging in a service learning project, complete with a report and a presentation. In addition to other assignments, including an intense final exam, there were also six required texts including a reader (also known to Columbians as course books). These six books are:

W. E. B. Du Bois, *The Souls of Black Folk* (New York: Dover Publications, Inc., 1994).

Paula Giddings, *When and Where I Enter: The Impact of Black Women on Race and Sex in America* (New York: Bantam Books, 1984).

Vincent Harding, *There Is a River: The Black Struggle for Freedom in America* (New York: Harcourt Brace and Company, 1981).

Manning Marable and Leith Mullings, eds., *Let Nobody Turn Us Around: Voices of Resistance, Reform and Renewal: An African-American Anthology* (Lanham, Maryland: Rowman and Littlefield, 2000).

Juan Williams, *Eyes on the Prize: America's Civil Rights Years, 1954-1965* (New York: Penguin, 1988).

Introduction to African American Studies: A Reader (course pack)

Each week had a theme for the lecture and the discussion, and the above readings were selected to present that theme textually. The course also included "suggested visual and internet resources," and many of the films listed were either accessible at the school library, the New York Public Library, or the Institute for Research in African American Studies at Columbia University (from which the class was offered). This course, like many at my research site, was held twice a week at 75-minute slots. It is important to note that, at this institution, African American/Black Studies is both a major and minor area of study. Knowing this, students may follow an outlined trajectory of courses as opposed to taking courses that do not connect and do not offer separate lecture and discussion sections. Other programs, where only three classes are required to qualify for a minor or certificate in the field (such as the research site I used for this project), struggle both to introduce the topic at its beginnings and create a continuum to link the conversation to Black Studies in its contemporary state. There simply is not enough time allotted in this type of structure. However, all introduction classes, even at schools where requirements are sometimes one to three courses, must include important and impactful historical presentations in the field in order to situate students as part of the political endeavor which is Black Studies.

Distributing Black Studies

When Black Studies programs fail to examine the threats against them, and to combat such threats by creating opportunities for students and faculty, the danger grows increasingly overbearing, as faculty members are left to scramble among the sprinkling of students. Some faculty members feel it is beneath them to create and distribute flyers of courses they are offering. They suggest that if students want to take it, they will register for it, and marketing is not a requirement for teaching. To some degree, this marketing methodology is time-consuming; if not done creatively, it could take away from the goal of Black Studies itself. However, when Black Studies programs are in an environment where it is not a major but a minor area of study, and the student population at large is limited in their interest, the threat becomes imminent.

When Black Studies is not a requirement but is classified or coated under names such as "Cultural Studies" or "Ethnic Studies," particularly at the research site and at schools many of the workshop students attended, the penalties of class closures are three-fold. In an open dialogue with a group of workshop students who were thinking about taking Black Studies classes at my research site, many suggested that: (1) faculty members whose classes closed due to low enrollment set a tone among the students that the class or the faculty member is in some way inadequate, creating much anxiety when offered again in subsequent semesters; (2) students who register for classes that end up closing lose opportunities to re-register for other classes (where seats fill quickly), and thus jeopardize their tuition payments (whether supported by financial aid or not); and (3) faculty members are also penalized for class closures in that they begin a deficit of teaching hours that are no longer in their control.

For Black Studies programs that are under constant threat, these types of situations are not only inevitable but are an impediment to the overall cultural function of the school; as such, they present such a disservice to the students. In some past years, I too have had to create flyers and have had to distribute them to various student-led organizations while promoting classes on school radio shows, developing blogs, and finding listservs to join to send out announcements of new courses. I have also hosted meet-and-greet events where Black Studies students (potentials and repeats) can not only meet each other but engage with me before the class. This has proven extremely successful in that after meeting students and hearing about their interests in the field, I am able to revisit my syllabus and reconstruct what I have assigned in order to address everyone's curiosity about specific topics. Their response to these revised syllabi is one of not gratitude but of satisfaction. While this may seem time-consuming, as part of a Black Studies department and among the students who have a sincere interest/passion in the field, these are concrete examples of communal-classroom building.

In many ways, hosting these events both on and off campus revitalizes the work of activists like Huey P. Newton, Bobby Seale, and many of the student activists of the San Francisco State University Strike in 1968. Organized in the communal model is a collective of students (not just Black) who begin to understand the political stakes of Black Studies and the importance of such a class, program, and field to them and the overall learning climate. It gives the students a sense of living in the historical scenarios which they are either studying or will soon embark on.

Reading Black Studies

In some introduction courses, professors may find it easier to assign enormous readers. In such texts, selections of writings in Black Studies are in abundance and thus present an overarching set of information from various perspectives. This may work well, particularly for survey courses. However, the downside of using just a reader is the lack of continuous interest from the majority of students. They tote around these mammoth books every week and sometimes fail to make connections to their lives and their learning experiences. Although sometimes expensive as well (if the student is not a recipient of book vouchers or financial aid), these readers need to be coupled or supplemented with other materials in order to present a timeline in the field.

Throughout my teaching career, I have always looked for creative ways to disseminate information among the students. For example, one semester, students looked at the syllabus and immediately became anxious at the amount of reading that was assigned. While some were restless about having to read "so much," others were worried about how they would be able to buy "so many books" for just one class. The school library held no copies of any of the books I assigned and arranging deliveries through interlibrary loans would only be more time consuming. Second, assigning only selections of individual books was at the top of the complaint list by students who felt they spent their money on books they did not read completely, at least not for class. This is another area where the work of communal-class may be successfully employed. By using the method of communal-class (which I continue to tweak), it becomes easier to find ways of making sure every student has what they need, regardless of financial situation, living circumstances, or time constraints. I asked the class if they would all agree to pooling their funds for supplies should their "copy money" run out. Their school gave them $100 in photocopying allocation (embedded in their tuition fees), and should it run out, every other print or copy job would be out of pocket. If their money was not used up by the end of the semester, it would also not be returned to them. Class reading assignments for many of them were additional costs (if not on aid). In the pool system for the communal-class model, a student was designated as the "collector." This student would collect one to two dollars from each classmate to cover the cost of a single case of paper (sometimes as cheap as $30–$35). Sometimes reams of paper would be donated to me for my projects and thus would be used for my classes. This ream/case would then be used solely for their readings, where I would make the copies for them. If any money should be left over, sometimes lunch/dinner was purchased for the class, or the class would agree that any one student struggling to purchase a book for the class would be granted their "wish." While this system may not seem directly connected to Black Studies, it illustrates the idea that Black Studies historically was a collective that sought to educate as its main agenda. By providing students with all of the tools necessary for them to excel in this field, the goal becomes easier to accomplish. The communal-class model is also a way of revisiting those examples of Black Studies traditions and inviting the students to participate in their own learning process/experience.

The fund-pooling also allowed students to access all the assigned materials with ease, which gave them a sense of organization and cooperation (Freire, 1970) and also encouraged them to pursue other reading materials in the field without or consideration of cost. With the more costly readers, students shared the cost of books, purchasing single used copies and finding innovative methods to share information (e.g., locating copies of the book online for free). All types of academic skills were in full force by using this method. This was especially important to graduate students who needed their funds to supply the early-childhood classrooms where they taught[2], and to undergraduates whose families were barely making ends meet. Books were luxuries some could not afford, and at a time when even the public libraries are at risk of closing, creative methodologies is a must. Together, we would find ways to make sure everyone was reading everything they were asked to and that they were inspired to read outside of the classroom as well.

Listed here are books that I have used in a variety of my Black Studies courses that have had tremendous impacts on my students. They are not all "traditional" texts, adapting to the idea that many of the students are organic and not traditional learners (Bernard-Carreño, 2010). Some titles were suggested by students, which I introduced in subsequent classes through pool-funded copies. It would be impossible to list all of the books I have ever used over 10 years of teaching Black Studies, but these are just a few that students can begin to consider as they gain curiosity about the field:

ASSIGNED BOOK SAMPLE:

Beck, Robert. *The Naked Soul of Iceberg Slim*. Los Angeles, CA: Holloway House Publishing Company, 1971.

Bernard, Regina Andrea. *Black & Brown Waves: The Cultural Politics of Young Women of Color and Feminism*. Boston: Sense Publishers, 2009.

Bloom, Harold. *Zora Neale Hurston's* Their Eyes Were Watching God. New York: Chelsea House Pub, 1987.

Cruse, Harold. *Crisis of the Negro Intellectual*. New York: Morrow, 1967.

Du Bois, W. E.B. *The Souls of Black Folk*. New York: Dover Publications, Inc., 1994.

hooks, bell. *We Real Cool: Black Men and Black Masculinity*. New York: Routledge, 2004.

Joseph, Peniel E. *Waiting 'til the Midnight Hour: A Narrative History of Black Power in America*. New York: Holt, 2007.

Karenga, Maulana. *Introduction to Black Studies*. Los Angeles: University of Sankore Press, 2002.

Marable, Manning, ed. *The New Black Renaissance: The Souls Anthology of Critical African-American Studies*. Boulder, CO: Paradigm, 2005.

McGruder, Aaron. *The Boondocks, Because I Know You Don't Read the Newspapers*. Kansas City, MO: Andrews McMeel Publishing, 2000.

Newton, Huey P., J. Herman Blake, and Fredrika Newton. *Revolutionary Suicide*. New York: Penguin Classics, 2011.

Noguera, P. A. *The Trouble with Black Boys, and Other Reflections on Race, Equity, and the Future of Public Education*. San Francisco: Jossey-Bass, 2009.

Sapphire. *Push, a Novel*. New York: Vintage, 1996.

Sertima, Ivan Van. *They Came Before Columbus, The African Presence in Ancient America*. 1st. Piscataway, NJ: Random House, 2003.

Sinclair, April. *Coffee Will Make You Black*. New York: Harper, 1995.

Souljah, Sister. *The Coldest Winter Ever, a Novel*. New York: Pocket, 2000.

Tatum, B. D. *Why Are All the Black Kids Sitting Together in the Cafeteria?* New York: Basic Books, 2003.

X, Malcolm, and Alex Haley. *The Autobiography of Malcolm X*. New York: Grove Press, 1966.

Besides the texts I have listed here,[3] I also introduce the students to Black Studies—specific databases, journals, and other online resources that they should know about, in order to further their study both during and after their time in class. In this model, I extend the module to outside of the classroom, where students and I have taken "field trips" to places like the New York Public Library's Schomburg Center for Research in Black Culture, located in Central Harlem. At the Schomburg, students learn about Arturo Schomburg's love for books but also his role in cultural politics as an Afro-Latino and a major figure in Harlem's power structure of literacy, education, and politics.

We have also visited other historical sites in Harlem and around New York, and have spent time together after the trips sharing meals at Black-owned restaurants. We have visited other community centers and businesses, including bookstores within the five boroughs. The students are encouraged to locate new places for visiting and add them to our ongoing database of Black Studies Sites for Study. These sites are later used in subsequent classes as service-learning hubs or sites of research. (More of this is discussed in chapter 6).

Sample of Projects

1. Personal Narrative Research Paper

In my second book *Nuyorganics: Organic Intellectualism, the Search for Racial Identity, and Nuyorican Thought* (2010), I introduce examples of simple entrance or introductory assignments, such as the Personal Narrative. In this essay/narrative, students are introducing me to who they are both in and out of the classroom and sharing with me candid information about their lived experience. I use this same introductory assignment to develop formal research papers. For example, my Black Studies students complete the narrative, but it is re-written as a "research paper" where their own life experiences and their pursuit for Black Studies–related knowledge are at the center of the research and ultimately used as the research subject. The students are essentially writing formal research papers about their lives and their experiences as related to Black Studies (whether they identify as Black or other) while including the assigned readings used during the semester. This assignment has proven successful for students who would not otherwise have an opportunity to decode their own understanding of the self as it relates to learning (Bernard-Carreño, 2010). Instead of traditional "grading" on a first round of reading these papers, I generally respond to the pieces by asking in-depth questions about particular events in their lives and asking larger questions about their learning experiences. Students are then given an opportunity to respond to the questions in a revised version of the paper.

I have found that with this particular assignment, students are fully immersed in the reading and find critical ways to locate places and points in the material where they agree or disagree with the author but most importantly make relative connections to themselves and the class. I also continue to find that with this personal narrative research paper, the students are responding directly to key ideas, asking questions of themselves, the author, and the general state of our community structures and processes. It begins to inspire the students without a prescribed prompt to seek opportunities for developing community-projects as you will read in the final chapter of this book.

THE NON-BLACK EXPERIENCE

Because I have always taught a racially diverse set of students (even in Black Studies), I have created writing assignments that ask students who are not Black to make comparisons to their lived experience and the reading. For many immigrant students, their sense of international struggle has been a driving force in the connection between their lived experience and Black Studies. Derived from their experience in the class is a sense of belonging where otherwise their connection to

Black identity would be amiss or not pertinent to the discussion. To this end, these students who are not Black tend to lead discussions as experts in their own "field," where students have learned about cultures far removed (as they tend to believe) from their own.

For example, one semester, an Asian (Korean) student made clear connections to Black identity by writing and designing his project about biracial Koreans (half Black, half Asian). The student discussed one famous Korean singer in particular who is half Black and half Korean but sings mostly in her native language. So often, students immediately think of biracial referring to half white and half Black (such as the case with President Barack Obama), that they forget there are other narratives as well. When this student presented the case for Afro-Korean identity, classmates were mesmerized and inspired to seek out other Black and biracial groups who have been marginalized by mainstream dialogue about race and/or Black-specific identity.

West Indian and Caribbean students have been similar in that many are uncomfortable with being identified as "African American" or "Black" and have found a number of ways to introduce their classmates to race and culture "on the island." Through language, music, religion, dance, dress, forms of schooling, and family structures, these students have not only introduced classmates to their own narratives but have also found ways to make connections to "other Blacks" who they would normally not associate with solely based on racial solidarity.

2. Bookshop Discovery

Returning to the ever-evolving issue with books and bookstores that fail to provide a continuum for learning about Black Studies, I have developed and use quite frequently a project called "Bookshop Discovery." In this project, students are asked to investigate both small and large bookstores in their neighborhoods and to examine whether or not "Black identity" or "Black knowledge" is available in plain-sight display or whether "Black books" hidden among more "popular" titles. The students are also urged to investigate bookstores in the vicinity of their school or other bookstores that pride themselves on independence from large chains.

At the exchange of much suspicion by bookstore owners and employees, the students found en masse that they almost always either had to look for themselves on the shelves, or find books about them that were stereotypical and/or voyeuristic. Students produced an enormous amount of research as to the lack of Black books in a number of bookstores in New York and began to develop ideas on how to begin addressing the issue in the community and with the bookstores themselves.

3. Community-Based Projects

For years, I have urged my students to engage in service learning opportunities outside of the classroom, as it was always a requirement of the actual coursework already. Due to lack of funding and institutional support, I have often found it a struggle to take large groups of students outside of New York in order to give them an example of applying classroom learning to "the field" away from home.[4] Opportunities for service have had to be created locally alongside grassroots organizations and movements.

In 2009, I created an assignment where students had to either plan and construct a Black Studies program for teens and/or college students or design a culturally responsive literacy program that was based in Black identity. While strenuous, rigorous, and time consuming, these projects built a sense of community, friendship, and solidarity among the students. As they worked toward a common goal of building programs that would present Black Studies in diverse ways, groups began to use their own lived experiences, personal narratives, hopes, and desires for their own futures. However, after spending an entire semester learning about the dismal effects of public education for Black and Latino/a children, the students began to think of their programs and workshop developments as panaceas to the problem.

Below, I list the guidelines I created for the project's direction and the questions students are required to answer. While it was mandatory to follow these questions and directions structurally, students were encouraged to list the questions they came up with during their research that they felt were important to the overall function of their group work.

4. Black Studies Program

Your goal as a group is to design a Black Studies program/workshop for either college and/or high school students. Having chosen your theme, your team should consider working on, researching, and presenting the following:

1. What do colleges need to offer students when it comes to Black Studies? (Is it a required class, an academic major, or a school club?) Make a clear argument for why it should be any of the areas you choose, and defend your position using historical examples in comparison to your own project.
2. What do high schools (if this is what you choose) need to offer students when it comes to Black Studies? (Is it a class, a major, or an after-school workshop?)

3. What kinds of classes/workshops should your program offer (depending on how many people are on your team, offer a class/workshop per team member)? These classes/workshops must be within your theme.
4. Faculty/teacher recruitment for such a program. Who will teach these classes and/or workshops? Offer job descriptions for each role, considering the work of prominent Black Studies scholars of the past while bringing current skill sets into the description.
5. What kind of student population are you trying to attract into the program, and how will you select them? Use Dr. Beverly Daniel Tatum's theoretical structure to answer how you include racial classifications to the address the needs of your participants. Make sure that your rationale for recruitment of particular groups is strongly defended and enough evidence is presented in favor/support of your selection criteria.
6. How long will the classes/workshops be?
7. Describe each class/workshop's content and rationale for each.
8. How much would each class/workshop cost?
    a. Work out your costs down to the penny.
    b. Include supplies necessary to execute the class/workshop successfully.
    c. What readings/materials for the workshop/class will you offer, and how will students access such materials?
    d. Raise the Money! Given the fact that many schools are "cutting back," and community organizations are also losing their funding, your team should prevent this by working out how much the program/workshop will cost and a clear, concise, and viable way to get the funds to run it.
9. How is your program political? How does it resemble the spirit of the Civil Rights movement, the Black Power movement, and more contemporary student-led movements?
    a. You must use our course readings (you may also use additional readings) to help you identify where your program falls (using key terms and ideas).
10. How will you evaluate the work of your students/workshop participants?
    a. What kinds of projects/work will the class do?
    b. How do you gauge the success and failure of your program?
11. Service: Your project must include a service learning component. By now, you have read the definition of service learning, and perhaps understand a bit of how it works as a historical element of Black Studies across our nation. Create a project of service for your Black Studies program. Whether undergrads or high school students participating, your write-up needs to explain how it will work. To really get a better idea, you may wish to communicate with an existing community organization (I have a

list you may start to use) to find out how your program relates to theirs and how you can work with them or create a program of service.

CONSIDER THIS
1. Your program must be NYC–based and consider all of the hubs/sites of research that are available to your group. You may include additional state trips as an add-on to your project.
2. Your program must either be for college or high school (choose one).
3. Your program must have a reading list based on the theme/content of the classes and workshops but generated or stemming from the readings of our class.
4. Your overall assignment/project must have a bibliography both for your workshops and for the assignment itself.
5. There are no page-length requirements for the paper portion of this project; as long as you hit the key points, work cohesively with your group, and work competitively, diligently and creatively, I expect that your project will be successful beyond your own expectations.
6. Throughout the semester, portions of the assignment will be due for review (in working draft format).

Building a Culturally Responsive Literacy Program
Project Goals

Your goal as a group is to build a Culturally Responsive Literacy Program (CRLP). Through the readings this semester, you will begin to identify what being culturally responsive is, but a good starting point is to consider Paulo Freire, Beverly Daniel Tatum, bell hooks, Stanley Aronowitz, Anna Julia Cooper, and Harold Cruse's work, where they clearly illustrate the responsibilities of advocacy through critical pedagogy methodologies. How you define "culturally responsive literacy" is totally up to your group. This can mean wellness programming, sustainability, Black nationalism/solidarity, Black farming, poverty, green planning/markets, traditional academic subjects, readings (fiction, nonfiction), or art/craft(s) techniques for survival—all embedded in historical references, of course. Your options are endless, and the more creative you are, the better and the more competitive your project.

The key here is to ask your team the following question: "what kind of topic is culturally responsive and can also inspire critical literacy, that which will allow learners to expand their intellectual capabilities, be excited about learning, and thus drive up their learning scores and experiences (particularly for younger learners)?" That's my question to your team—now it's your turn to answer it by building your program.⁵

What derived from just these two assignments were entire programs, complete with funding requirements and creative ways to access such funding. These projects were based on Black political and historical identity infused with current needs of various communities in New York City. Topics ranged from:

1. Black male dialogue training: inspired by a student whose best friend who was murdered, her commitment to preserving his memory, and her dedication to anti-violence programming.
2. The relationship of Blacks and Latino/as living in shared communities, as presented through the work of Black and Latino/a sororities and fraternities.
3. Financial literacy programs for Black youth living in impoverished households and larger communities suffering from economic pitfalls.
4. Hip Hop and urban poetry workshops to inspire critical literacy and positive Black identity.
5. High school drop-out prevention programs.
6. Sexual health programs targeted at college students and inclusive of adolescent and teen girls' sexual health.
7. Reading programs creating diverse reading groups around Black writing and young writers of color.

As you can see, the ideas were quite numerous, and it would be impossible to mention all the projects produced by my students over the years. However, through this communal-class methodology and introduction to the relationship between the student, the self, and the community they learn about, students of Black Studies are allowed to get more in depth with their academic material. This can also be achieved by working towards a number of visible results among Black Studies undergraduates:⁶

1. Understand the political and racially charged history of Black Studies.
2. Find a personal and collegiate identity and connection to the readings assigned.
3. Have complete access to the breadth of information on Black Studies.
4. Work collectively towards a common and larger societal goal.
5. See their own lived experiences reflected in the work they do in such a course.
6. Relate Black Studies courses not only to their life experiences outside of school but make clear use of their major areas of study in relation to their Black Studies courses.

7. Find solidarity and comfort in the class in order to share, express, and convey deep and candid feelings about the topics and each other.
8. Are given multiple ways of consuming and thus producing the knowledge pertinent to Black Studies and their lived experience.
9. Continue to work to keep Black Studies afloat: whether they are pursuing a major, minor, or certificate in the field and whether they are at an Ivy League, public college or community-based program.
10. Take their Black Studies class back into their communities in a variety of ways.

CHAPTER SIX

Scholarship and Community

Throughout this book, I have argued that Black Studies must and can ensure its longevity through sincere integration, cooperation, and involvement with not only the academic setting it is housed in but within and among the Black community where it has been so deeply rooted and within and among the community enveloping the university/college. In this chapter I present another set of concrete examples and a detailed analysis of projects that speak directly to the task of strengthening the relationship between Black Studies and the university. In addition to this analysis, this chapter examines and presents how full integration with university and community can undeniably build strong programming and stronger, more well-rounded students in this and other fields.

Historically, Black Studies has always included a worker–thinker dual personality. When students were protesting for the inclusion of Black Studies programs in institutions of higher learning, they also wanted a place where they could produce scholarship in the field while presumably providing active community service. Rogers (2008) argues that Black Studies is no longer inclusive of the community. He writes,

> It appears that the more the discipline has become institutionalized, the more its humanistic component has dissipated from the scene (Rogers, 1120).

Rogers' assertions, at some schools, would be hard to disprove. While his declaration may not be accurate for every Black Studies program, it was accurate at the 163 institutions of higher learning that he examined (Rogers, 1128), and it was accurate at my research site as well. Both Rogers and other researchers in the field support the argument I make that service-learning is a major route to building this connection between academia and community, and reintegrating students into the historical frame of Black Studies.

I suggest that service-learning does more than just make a connection between academia and community. These opportunities that connect the classroom to the world around us increase academic and self-discipline, developmental learning (even at the adult stages of life), social skills, self-esteem, and a connection to reality outside of an assigned reading and/or ethnographic tale. For Black Studies students, the connection is even more significant and essential because it is rooted in a narrative of both history of social service, holding an even deeper meaning for those involved in its work. George Edmund Haynes, an educator and social worker, has been credited with designing one of the first service-learning/experiential learning courses connected to Black Studies (at Fisk University).

> Haynes' interest in racial uplift, self-help initiatives, and education to improve conditions of black people led him to develop a course of instruction that provided black students with systematic knowledge about their race and sensitive appreciation of pressing social problems in their community. The course was designed so students could utilize social science knowledge and skills in field experience and service in the black community. It was, in effect, an internship with both a service and reflection component, in which students were expected to learn from their subjects and gain insight from their community involvement. The students in this exchange would share their academic knowledge with the community by identifying problems, utilizing social science skills, and participating in problem solving with the community (Carlton-La Ney, 1983)

In 2008, Rogers presented a proposal for a Black Studies curriculum that could attempt to do what Haynes had created in his vision of experiential learning. Rogers also suggests that his proposal could easily be integrated into any Black Studies curriculum that requires a service-learning component. Where Rogers and I differ is in the presentation of such an idea. While his proposal recommends discrete service-learning based courses, to avoid a potential university debate about available funding and a revamping of an entire existing curriculum (perceived as troublesome or time-consuming and downright "impossible" for some), I propose that service-learning be integrated into each Black Studies class and that a single seminar on service learning be a program requirement.[1] If all faculty members are involved in the service-learning model, it is less likely that one professor would be singled out for requiring too much individual or singular course-funding.

In addition, models of service-learning requirements can and should change, depending on the level of ability and the population of the class. For example, the integrated service-learning model that I am proposing here could be fully included in the three courses required for the Black Studies minor program that I examined for this research. A seminar solely focusing on service learning in Black Studies can easily generate its own area of study. Thus, students both majoring and minoring in Black Studies would be receiving more content and community in their Black Studies classes and are ultimately spending more time in the community as a research site/hub. For graduate students pursuing masters and doctorates in the field of Black Studies, the service-learning component would then again be revamped.

Here I will describe my proposal for a required service learning component within the frame of a three-class requirement for a minor offered by the institution which I chronicled for this research project. Courses that were taught twice a week ran for 75 minutes per session for 16 weeks. If the courses met once a week, they were taught for 3 hours a session, also for 16 weeks. Either format can accommodate the module I am proposing, utilizing the communal-class model that I described in Chapter 5.

"Introduction to Black Studies" was a course offered during my chronicling project/research, but this particular course was not required as part of the minor (although some of the more advanced courses did require the course as a prerequisite). The "Introduction" course carried no required readings or trajectory; rather, it themed-based around the professor's decided structure. The three courses required for the minor also follow no pattern and thus seem to be part of a potpourri of Black Studies ideas as opposed to concentrated path of navigation that attempt to build a solid foundation of information and training.

Having participated in the program through research and practice, it is fair to say that although there have been some cosmetic changes to the department/program, the curriculum has stayed the same. Changes have occurred regarding the turnover rates of Black Studies professors in the department, courses being taught under specializations, and professors who have taken the time to give existing courses new faces (during class). However, a complete overhaul and facelift of course offerings have not taken place, and in the 10 years of research and review, the courses still follow no pattern to completion or complete understanding of Black Studies.

Ideally, more courses should be required to complete the minor, but if that is not in the near future for this particular program, the social and academic responsibilities of the coursework ultimately fall on educators. This risks what Drake states comes with the penalty of faculty reducing "their chances of success in the competition for recognition through publication" (Drake, 1979, 14) by working endlessly in developing, maintaining, and running service-learning courses alongside their students. If the department itself does not envision mass changes to the curriculum, faculty must work together to revamp their own courses with new ideas while protecting the history of Black Studies as a social movement. Faculty must also work together in community models themselves in order to create and safeguard the communal class so that one professor does not bear the entire weight of a studying population, particularly while these efforts are under-funded or not funded at all. Service-learning opportunities must be created, which students can pursue within any Black Studies faculty member's course or independently. This proposed set of course construction and ideas is designed for this particular program in mind (three-course minor) but can be tweaked and re-applied to any level of Black Studies program.

Course 1: Introduction to Black Studies & Service Learning

To begin the stream of Black Studies & Service Learning model that I am proposing, "Introduction to Black Studies" would be a required course for the minor. Every Fall semester, the Introduction class would be offered. It would not only survey and analyze the various and diverse histories of Black Studies, its programs, its scholars, and its current status but would introduce students to the beginnings of service-learning in Black Studies. As Rogers argues,

> In terms of Black education, there is at least a century-long legacy of service learning. According to Stevens (2003), they were initiated first in the Black churches and colleges (Rogers, 1125).

How then can service-learning be eliminated from contemporary forms of Black Studies training, whether at the undergraduate or graduate level? Stemming from such a rich history, Black Studies service-learning should find an easy home in an "Introduction to Black Studies" course.

In this proposed Introduction, Black women as pioneers of service-learning in the discipline would be examined. Its use in this course could easily be marketed for cross-listing in other disciplines and academic programs/departments, such as Women's Studies or a version of Multicultural Studies, thus attracting a larger, more diverse population of students.

> Many of the women believed that the best way to create a viable black community and to reform society was to educate, instruct, and care for the

young and elderly, so they engaged in teaching, social work, and other communal efforts (Osofsky, 1965; Reid, 1995).

Students in the "Introduction to Black Studies" class would study the community and activist contributions of women like Janie Porter Barrett of the Black Women's Social Club, Marcy Church Terrell, Anna Julia Cooper, Jane Edna Hunter, and Ida B. Wells-Barnett as a starting point of both Black Studies and Black Studies service-learning examples. Too often these women and women of similar background are only sporadically discussed in Women's Studies, Multicultural Studies, and History courses. These women in particular were major forces in Black service-learning through institutions of higher learning as well as community organizations and other types of "clubs."

> Through their actions, they intended to promote social change and strengthen the internal social order of community. With this mindset and emphasis on using citizenship, democracy, and unity in the race, black women seemed to embrace the service-learning philosophy in programs and social action rather than as a formal education approach (Stevens, 2003).

Although notable scholar and political commentator Melissa Harris-Perry founded the Anna Julia Cooper Project at Tulane University[2] and has an extensive syllabus for a class she teaches on "Black Women's Political Activism,"[3] courses that teach Cooper's work seem sporadic. After a detailed search through the syllabi of Black Studies courses, coverage of her work seemed very limited.

The analysis of these early pioneers in Black Studies service-learning would give students a historical framework from which they can design their own service learning project. For example, Dr. Cooper focused a lot of her community time and academic work around social settlement houses and women's welfare activism. She viewed both these as avenues to "uplift the race." Much as I have been referred to as an "activist-educator," students in the module of Black Studies that I present here could easily adopt a self-definition as "student activist," staying sincere and authentic to the field, whether they are pursuing it at the minor, major, undergraduate or graduate level(s). Students in current Black Studies courses can also easily develop service-learning projects at sites similar to where Dr. Cooper did much of her work and research. Such sites still exist today and address a multitude of social problems, particularly in New York City.

Having studied the rich history of Black Studies and experiential learning/service-learning in this first course, students would be required to produce:

(1) a formal proposal, which would present the professor and the rest of the class with his/her interest in a particular topic within the confines of what was studied for 16 weeks. Versions of this proposal could also include topics that were not discussed in the class at length but that were sparked by discussions and readings. Students could choose to work alone for their proposal submission or on a team of sorts. (2) Over holiday break (November–end of December/early January), students would be required to fine-tune their proposals and meet with their Black Studies advisor at least once (of course, in keeping with technology, students would have the option of "meeting" digitally as well). After polishing their proposal, students would then be ready to embark on the second course in the minor sequence, where they would use their proposal as a guide to securing a physical research site or Black Studies research hub for the second semester. This site or hub would have to meet the goals designed by the department and would be agreed upon by faculty and student.

Course No. 2: Black Studies: Area of Specialty

During the Spring semester, faculty members would teach a variety of courses that would meet the following student needs: develop their research proposal, build on the "Introduction to Black Studies" class, and prepare them for the final "Black Studies and Community" course in the third semester. Depending on what students would have focused on in the "Introduction to Black Studies" course, these specialty courses would reflect the interest not only of the students but of the faculty members who would now have the opportunity to teach areas within their expertise and areas of interest. One or two sections of the "Introduction to Black Studies" course may also be re-offered for students who enter the program late or find their interest after the Fall semester. As with Rogers' suggestion, this second course proposed here (which I have titled "Black Studies: Areas of Specialty") would also "require the participants to serve a minimum number of hours per week at a community organization" (Rogers, 1131). Since the site of research used for this book housed a majority of commuter-students who held part-time or full-time jobs off-campus, the hours spent at the community organization would be based on the project the student is working on, designated by the organization and approved by the faculty advisor.

Sample Specialty Course

An example of a second course offering could be similar to an undergraduate course I have taught in the past, "Selected Problems in the Black Community." This course offered my students a wide variety of topics that were easily disbursed for diverse conversation and scholarly investigation yet also allowed for a collective research focus on one topic: "Hunger, Food Shortage, and Poverty in Black Communities." Although this course was part of the potpourri of offerings within the Black Studies program and was open to anyone who needed it, was interested in it, or simply needed to fill a gap in their schedule, I was able to use the course to pilot my service-learning module in one semester. Since a good majority of the students had never taken the department's "Introduction to Black Studies" course, I had to include the introductory information, which proved challenging to do respectfully in just 16 weeks. After two weeks of introducing the pedagogical history and narratives of Black Studies service-learning, we began to discuss the designated "Selected Problems in the Black Community." Since the course was a secondary-level course, it offered a survey of such "selected problems" within the theme of "Hunger, Food Shortage, and Poverty in Black Communities" that I sketched thematically for them.

After spending just a few short weeks discussing the plight of Black communities nationally and internationally, students were shocked to find that hunger and food shortage affected Black communities right in New York. Due to accessibility, use, abuse, and all types of underground markets that deal with food security, students were under the impression that low-income communities (particularly Black communities) were at no risk for hunger. As the semester progressed, students began to understand how food travels to our plates, who eats what, and how various Black communities throughout New York City struggle to eat every day (particularly children). Eating healthily in Black communities was another big area of discussion and research among the students. After the initial shock at such a discovery, students began to develop their research proposals in very creative ways. Still focusing on "selected problems" as the course dictated, but under the theme of "Hunger, Food Shortage and Poverty in Black Communities," students began pairing up to discover even more information. Some of the topics that students designed for research included:

1. Homeless Black United States veterans and the lack of food Access upon return from combat.
2. Homeless shelters, Black males, and food distribution.
3. Black populations at soup kitchens.
4. Black populations at food pantries.
5. Black single mothers and difficulty in providing food for their infants and toddlers.
6. Social welfare programs that hurt, not help, Black communities.
7. Food access in low-income Black neighborhoods (bodegas, fast food restaurants, etc.).
8. Healthy food invisibility in poor Black (and Latino/a) neighborhoods.

While there are more, those were some of the topics that produced the best results and projects. Students spent weeks researching their topics but also used their findings to build centers of information (more of this explained in course 3 below). In addition, since students were contextualizing the reading and really beginning to understand the struggle of Black families in New York City's low-income neighborhoods (or the homeless for that matter) in accessing food, I developed relationships with various soup kitchens, food banks, and food pantries all throughout the city for students to volunteer at while using the site as a research hub. While volunteering at these sites/research hubs, the students not only gained a sense of leadership and sense of community involvement, they also developed activist and advocate voices that helped to fuel political decisions that the general public fails to consider.

At the end of this second course, students were required to work on traditional research papers of standard length (20–25 pages) based on their topic and fieldwork accomplished during the semester, carefully remembering to incorporate the historical frameworks of Black Studies service-learning. However, where in other "traditional" classes, these types of formal research papers would usually be an individual assignment, under the communal-class method, students on research teams could produce one group paper with the inclusion of all of their individual research. Although there were basic formal examinations along the way to keep names, dates, and theories sharp throughout the course, the final requirement for this second class was to turn in their research and spend the summer volunteering at one of the visited sites. Again, the hours of volunteering would be at the behest of the organization and agreed upon by faculty advisor and student. The time spent at some of these organizations during my course has led to permanent volunteer positions, part-time, and full-time jobs. Where it did not lead to such volunteer opportunities or paid employment, it certainly led to a stronger resume and community networking.

Off-Time Research

During the summer months, when students were taking Black Studies classes as electives,[4] many were invited to work as interns on several projects that I was involved in (particularly around race and food justice). These opportunities fulfill the requirement I have for writing letters of recommendation (especially because the three-course Black Studies service-learning program I describe in this chapter is one that I am designing for future use and offering a pilot version now in the jumble of classes I currently teach). In addition to interning for letters of recommendations for graduate school, other professional programs, and jobs, students who remained interested after the "Selected Problems" course were invited to continue volunteering to research the topic in a variety of ways. Students have written to me over the semesters where I have piloted this module and have thanked me for including them in this research endeavor but mostly for making them feel as part of a "small family," where "everyone knows everyone" and semesters later we all are still community via email or through blog posts. As with Haynes's model at Fisk, my own course as well "was conceived in the spirit of reciprocity" and

> the hope was that such intense involvement would instill in students a deeper appreciation for the plight of the race. This new appreciation would encourage students toward further social action (Stevens 2003).

Course No. 3: Black Studies and the Community

The third and final course, "Black Studies and Community," would review not only the proposed research of the first course and the research stage and the physical research/fieldwork stages of the second course but would also require a theoretical and as-practical-as-possible design of a new program that addresses the area of study that the student has been focusing on since the first course. Students in this final seminar will be required to create a functional program that would be housed in a community they have studied and that could also be used by new students just entering the minor program. Similar to Rogers and his version of a final course, which he titles "Management of Service Learning," "students would use their familiarity with service-learning that they gained by taking the previous service learning courses to assist the faculty in managing the students" (Rogers, 1131). The difference here is that Rogers proposes that students serve as faculty assistants and as student mentors, whereas my program proposes that students in the final course design a community program that new students can use as research hubs/sites.

The community programs being created by students are ideally to be housed in the community they seek to serve and should be aimed at directly addressing the social issues the students have been researching throughout the two prior courses, off-season volunteering, interning, and assisting in other ways. Although as previously mentioned, I have been working with Black Studies students for over 10 years in variations of service-learning modules that I have created, and although the students have created creatively superb programs, in this particular module that I am now proposing, service-learning projects would constantly be revamped for scholarly competitiveness. For example, if implemented now with the inclusion of Women Studies and Urban Studies students (as mentioned above in the potential Introduction course), project directions could include examples of program-design and community-relationship by way of Anna Julia Cooper's involvement with Frelinghuysen University in Washington, D.C. (founded in 1906) by Jesse Lawson. The

> educational center [Frelinghuysen] served as a group of schools intended to provide social services, religious training, and educational programs for the people who needed them most (Keller, 58).

Frelinghuysen has been deemed one of the earliest examples of community college, and it is surprising that many Black Studies students, whether at the community college or senior college level(s) do not know this or use her work extensively. Using Frelinghuysen as the primary example alongside their own research topics and training to date, students would be required to design their own "centers" that provide the educational, political, and social services they deem necessary to begin eradicating the social dilemma they have been studying.

The final endeavor in this course is for faculty and students to select students from the various final courses (in an established selection committee) and have them present their research, findings, and program/center design. Ultimately members/residents of the communities studied, leaders and members of relevant community organizations, and department/program faculty would be present at this colloquium or brown-bag lunch and discussion. At the time of my research, a new initiative was created at one of the universities that distributed financial awards for class-based "best research proposal." A similar method would be used in this module, although the presentation would include students from every one of the final courses in the department. Through presentation, discussion, and a collective voting process (under which strict guidelines would be issued), students with the most feasible program would be awarded the opportunity to pilot run their program/project at the community organization that is determined to be most in need. Securing this spot would come with a small research budget in order to institute and run the program for a designated amount of time, leaving work for subsequent students to fulfill as the program continues to grow.

While such a program may seem to require an abundance of institutional funds, the reality is that it requires primarily the dedication of faculty members in the field, affiliates of other departments who have a sincere and legitimate interest (Christian, 2007), the supported interest of students, and the building of partnerships with community leaders, members and organizations.

Bibliography

Allen, E.B. (2004). *Low Road: The Life and Legacy of Donald Goines*. New York: St. Martin's Press.
Allen, R.L. (1974). "Politics of the attack on Black Studies." *The Black Scholar*, *16*(6), 2–7.
Anderson, E. (1999). *Code of the Street: Decency, Violence, and the Moral Life of the Inner City*. New York: Norton.
Asante, M.K. (2005). "The Discipline of Africology at the Crossroads: Toward an Eshuean Response to Intellectual Dilemma." *Black Scholar*, 35.2. 37–49.
Baldwin, J. (1963). *The Fire Next Time*. 1st ed. New York: Vintage.
Baldwin, J. (2000). *Go Tell It on the Mountain*. New York: Dial Press.
Baraka, Imamu Amiri. (1997). *The Autobiography of LeRoi Jones*. Chicago: Chicago Review Press.
Beck, R. (1971). *The Naked Soul of Iceberg Slim*. Los Angeles: Holloway House.
Bernard, R.A. (2009). *Black & Brown Waves: The Cultural Politics of Young Women of Color and Feminism*. Boston: Sense Publishers.
Bernard-Carreño, R. (2010). *Nuyorganics, Organic Intellectualism, the Search for Racial Identity, and Nuyorican Thought*. New York: Lang.
Bloom, H. (1987). *Zora Neale Hurston's* Their Eyes Were Watching God. New York: Chelsea House Publishers.
Carlton La-Ney, I. (1983). "Notes on a Forgotten Black Sociologist and Social Worker: George Edmund Haynes." *Journal of Sociology and Social Welfare*, 10, 530–9.
Chelton, M.K. (2005). "Perspectives on YA Practice: Common YA Models of Service in Public Libraries: Advantages and Disadvantages." *Young Adult Library Services: The Journal of the Young Adult Library Services Association*, 3(4). 4–11.
Christian, M. (2007). "'Notes on Black Studies: Its Continuing Necessity in the Academy and Beyond." *Journal of Black Studies*, 37. 348–64.

Collins, P.H. (2000). *Black Feminist Thought, Knowledge, Consciousness, and the Politics of Empowerment*. 2nd ed. New York: Routledge.

Crane, S. (2005). *Maggie: A Girl of the Streets and Other Writings about New York*. New York: Barnes & Noble Classics.

Cruse, H. (1967). *Crisis of the Negro Intellectual*. New York: Morrow.

Cuyjet, M.J. (2006). *African American Men in College*. San Francisco: Jossey-Bass.

Dickerson, D. (2004). *The End of Blackness: Returning the Souls of Black Folk to Their Rightful Owners*. New York: Pantheon.

Dodson, A. P. (2006). "The Mainstreaming of Street Lit." *Black Issues Book Review*, 8(4), 6.

Drake, S.C. (1979). "What Happened to Black Studies?" *New York University Education Quarterly*, 10. 9–16.

Du Bois, W.E.B. (1994). *The Souls of Black Folk*. New York: Dover Publications, Inc.

Fialkoff, F. (2006). "Street lit takes a hit." *Library Journal*, February.

Fisher, M.T. (2009). *Black Literate Lives, Historical and Contemporary Perspectives*. New York: Taylor & Francis.

Ford, N. A. (1974). "White colleges and the future of black studies." In Norment, N. (ed.). *The African American Studies Reader* (pp. 585–592). Durham, NC: Carolina Academic Press.

Forman, M., and Neal, M. A. (2011). *That's the Joint: The Hip Hop Studies Reader*. 2nd edition. New York: Routledge.

Franklin, H. B. (2008). "Can the Penitentiary Teach the Academy How to Read?" *PMLA, 123*(3), 643–649.

Freire, P. (2000). *Pedagogy of the Oppressed*, 30th Anniversary Edition. New York: Continuum.

Gates, H.L. (1988). *The Signifying Monkey: A Theory of African-American Literary Criticism*. New York: Oxford University Press.

Giddings, P. (1984). *When and Where I Enter: The Impact of Black Women on Race and Sex in America*. New York: Bantam.

Gmelch, S. (1998). *Gender on Campus: Issues for College Women*. New Brunswick, NJ: Rutgers University Press.

Goines, D. (1971). *Dopefiend*. Los Angeles: Holloway House

Goines, D. (1972). *Whoreson*. Los Angeles: Holloway House.

Goines, D. (1973). *White Man's Justice, Black Man's Grief*. Los Angeles: Holloway House.

Harding, V. (1981). *There Is a River: The Black Struggle for Freedom in America* . New York: Harcourt Brace and Company.

Hare, N. (1972),."The Battle of Black Studies." *Black Scholar*, 3. 32–27.

Harvey, S. (2011). *Act Like a Lady, Think Like a Man: What Men Really Think about Love, Relationships, Intimacy, and Commitment*. New York: Amistad.

Haygood, M., E.M. Brown, R.J. McLean, and A. Burt-Murray. (2010). *The Little Black Book of Success, Laws of Leadership for Black Women*. New York: One World/Ballantine.

Haygood, W. (2011). *Sweet Thunder, The Life and Times of Sugar Ray Robinson*. Chicago: Lawrence Hill Books.

hooks, b. (1994). *Teaching to Transgress*. New York, NY: Routledge.

hooks, b. (2004). *We Real Cool: Black Men and Black Masculinity*. New York: Routledge.

hooks, b. (2006). *Outlaw Culture, Resisting Representations*. New York: Routledge.

Horton-Stallings, L. "'I'm Goin Pimp Whores!': The Goines Factor and the Theory of a Hip-Hop Neo-Slave Narrative." *CR: The New Centennial Review*, vol. 3, no. 3. 175–203.

Hurston, Z.N. (1937). *Their Eyes Were Watching God*. Philadelphia: J.B. Lippincott Co.
Jackson, G. (1994). *Soledad Brother: The Prison Letters of George Jackson*. Chicago: Lawrence Hill Books.
John, D., and D. Paisner. (2010). *The Brand Within: The Power of Branding from Birth to the Boardroom*. Display of Power Pub Inc.
Joseph, P. (2007). *Waiting 'Til the Midnight Hour: A Narrative History of Black Power in America*. New York: Holt.
Karenga, M. (2002). *Introduction to Black Studies*. Los Angeles: University of Sankore Press.
Keller, F. R. (1999). An educational controversy: Anna Julia Cooper's vision of resolution. *NWSA Journal*, 11(3), 49–67.
Kelley, R. (2010). *Thelonious Monk: The Life and Times of an American Original*. New York: Free Press.
Kelley, R. D.G. (1997). *Yo' Mama's Disfunktional!: Fighting the Culture Wars in Urban America*. Boston: Beacon Press.
Kennedy, E.M. (2010). *True Compass: A Memoir*. New York: Hachette Digital, Inc.
Kincheloe, J.L. (2001). *Getting Beyond the Facts, Teaching Social Studies/social Sciences in the Twenty-first Century*. New York: Lang.
KRS-One. (2009). *The Gospel of Hip Hop, The First Instrument*. New York: PowerHouse Books.
Larsen, N. (1986). *Quicksand*. New Brunswick: Rutgers University Press.
Lewis, O. (1966). *La vida: A Puerto Rican Family in the Culture of Poverty—San Juan and New York*. New York: Random House.
Marable, M. (1998). *Black Leadership*. New York: Columbia University Press.
Marable, M. (2000). *Dispatches from the Ebony Tower: Intellectuals Confront the African American Experience*. New York: Columbia University Press.
Marable, M. (2005). *The New Black Renaissance: The Souls Anthology of Critical African-American Studies*. Boulder, CO: Paradigm.
Marable, M., and L. Mullings. (2000). *Let Nobody Turn Us Around: Voices of Resistance*. Lanham, MD: Rowman and Littlefield.
McGruder, A. (2000). *The Boondocks: Because I Know You Don't Read the Newspapers*. Kansas City, MO: Andrews McMeel.
Moore, N. (2010). Sonia Sanchez on the State of Black Books. July 12. www.theroot.com/views/sonia-sanchez-state-black-books.
Murtadha, K., and D.M. Watts. (2005). "Linking the Struggle for Education and Social Justice: Historical Perspectives of African American Leadership in Schools." *Educational Administration Quarterly*, 41. 591–608.
Newton, H.P. (2009). *Revolutionary Suicide*. Reprint ed. New York: Penguin Classics.
Noguera, P.A. (2009). *The Trouble with Black Boys ... and Other Reflections on Race, Equity, and the Future of Public Education*. San Francisco: Jossey-Bass.
Norment, N. (2007). *The African American Studies Reader*. Durham, NC: Carolina Academic Press.
Osofsky, G. (1965). *Harlem: The making of a ghetto*. New York: Harper and Row Publishers.
Owens, B. (1979). "A New Beginning towards a More Productive Future for Black Studies." *Contributions in Black Studies*. 3, 39–43.
Quinn, E. (2001). *Media, Culture, and the Modern African American Freedom Struggle*. Gainesville, FL: University Press of Florida.
Reid, J. B. (1995). A career to build, a people to serve, a purpose to accomplish: Race, class, gender and Detroit's first black women teachers, 1865–1910. In
Rich, A. (1979). *On Lies, Secrets, and Silence: Selected Prose 1966–1978*. New York: Norton.

Rogers, I. (2010). "Required Service-Learning Courses: A Disciplinary Necessity to Preserve the Decaying Social Mission of Black Studies." *Journal of Black Studies*, 40. 1119–35.
Sapphire. (1996). *Push: A Novel*. New York: Vintage.
Sertima, I.V. (2003). *They Came before Columbus: The African Presence in Ancient America*. 1st. ed. Piscataway, NJ: Random House.
Signorelli, N. (1997). "Reflections of the Girls in the Media." *Fourth Annual Children & Media Conference*. 2–15.
Sinclair, A. (1995). *Coffee Will Make You Black*. New York: Harper.
Smith, D. (1997, May 1). "Media More Likely to Show Women Talking about Romance Than at a Job, Study Says." *The New York Times*.
Souljah, S. (2000). *The Coldest Winter Ever: A Novel*. New York: Pocket.
Stevens, C.S. (2003). "Unrecognized Roots of Service-Learning in African American Social Thought and Action, 1890–1930." *Michigan Journal of Community Service Learning*, 9. 25–34.
Stringer, V.M. (2007). *Dirty Red*. New York: Atria Books.
Tatum, B.D. (2003). *Why Are All the Black Kids Sitting Together in the Cafeteria?* New York: Basic Books.
University of Chicago Committee on Educational Television. (1953). "Television and the University." *The School Review*, 61(4). 202–25.
Walker, A. (1982). *The Color Purple*. New York: Harcourt Brace.
West, C. (2010). *Brother West, Living and Loving Out Loud: A Memoir*. New York: Smiley Books.
Williams, J. (1988). *Eyes on the Prize: America's Civil Rights Years, 1954–1965*. New York: Penguin.
Williamson, C., and T. Cluse-Tolar. (2002). "Pimp-controlled Prostitution: Still an Integral Part of Street Life." *Violence Against Women*, 8(9). 1074–1092.
Wright, R. (2008). *Black Boy*. New York: Harper Perennial Modern Classics.

Filmography

Abrams, J.J., prod. (1998). "Pilot." *Felicity*. The WB Television Network. Television.
Allen, D., dir. (1987). *A Different World*. National Broadcasting Company. Television.
Bunim, M., dir. (1992). *The Real World*. MTV Networks. Television.
Dylan, Jesse, dir. (2001). *How High*. Jersey Films. Film.
Fales, S., writer, D. Allen, dir., and M. Carsey, executive producer. (1991). "We've Only Just Begun." *A Different World*. National Broadcasting Company. Television.
Farquhar, R., writer. (1999). *The Parkers*. Television.
Fuqua, A., dir. (2001). *Training Day*. Warner Bros. Productions. Film.
Hagan, D., dir. (2008). *College*. Element Films. Film.
Kanew, J., dir. (1984). *Revenge of the Nerds*. Interscope Communications. Film.
Keshishian, A., dir. (1994). *With Honors*. Spring Creek Productions. Film.
Klein, D., dir. (2004). *College Hill*. Black Entertainment Television. Television.
Landis, J., dir. (1978). *Animal House*. Universal Pictures. Film.
McGee, S.A., writer, J. Melman, dir., and B. Boulware, executive producer. (1999.) "Grape Nuts." *The Parkers*. United Paramount Network. Television.
Miller, G.H., writer, D. Allen, dir., and M. Carsey, executive producer. (1991). "The Dwayne Mutiny." *A Different World*. National Broadcasting Company. Television.

Moseley, R., writer, K. Hardison, dir., and M. Carsey, executive producer. (1993). "Homie, Don't Ya Know Me?" *A Different World*. National Broadcasting Company. Television.
Nicks, D., dir. (2002). *Slackers*. Alliance Atlantis Communications. Film.
Pink, S., dir. (2006). *Accepted*. Universal Pictures. Film.
Rash, S., dir. (1993). *Son in Law*. Hollywood Pictures. Film.

Internet Resources

Adalian, J. (2009, November 09). "The CW Gives 'Life Unexpected' a 'Gossip Girl' boost." *The Wrap: Covering Hollywood*. Retrieved from http://www.thewrap.com/ind-column/cw-gives-life-unexpected-gossip-girl-boost-9877.
Arnzen, M. (2005, April 24). *Media Fasting*. Retrieved from http://blogs.setonhill.edu/MikeArnzen/009181.html.
Campbell, E. (N.d.). "20th Century Prison Literature." *Mount St Mar'ys Syllabus*. Retrieved from http://www.msmc.la.edu/PDFFiles/WCsyllabiarchive/Fall2003/eng192fa03.1u.pdf. Retrieved July 8, 2011.
"A Different World (TV series)." (2009, December 28). *Wikipedia, The Free Encyclopedia*. Retrieved from http://en.wikipedia.org/w/index.php?title=A_Different_World_(TV_series)&oldid=334565723. Retrieved October 22, 2009.
"Federal Work Study: Program Description." Retrieved from http://www.ed.gov/programs/fws/index.html. Retrieved October 22, 2009.
"A Felicity Page. Characters: Elena Tyler." (1999). Retrieved from http://www.felicitypage.com/elena.html. Retrieved October 22, 2009.
Gibbons, S. (2008). *Media Report to Women: Industry Statistics*. Retrieved from http://www.mediareporttowomen.com/statistics.htm.
Harris-Perry, M. (2012). "Black Women's Political Activism Syllabus." *Anna Julia Cooper Project Mission*. Newcomb College Institute of Tulane University, Fall 2012. Retrieved from http://cooperproject.org/wp-content/uploads/2012/07/BlackWomActivism-Syllabus.pdf. Retrieved 30 July 2012.
Marable, M. (2005). "Intro to African American Studies Syllabus." Columbia University. Retrieved from http://www.columbia.edu/cu/ccbh/pdfs/afamsyllabus2005.pdf. Retrieved November 15, 2010.
Morrissey, T.E. (2009, June 2). "20 Feminist TV Characters." *Jezebel*. Retrieved from http://jezebel.com/5274600/20-feminist-tv-characters.
Naison, M. (2009). "Hip Hop Street Literature Narratives." Retrieved from http://www.fordham.edu/images/academics/history_department/graduate_syllabus/f09_5050_naison.pdf. Retrieved April 6, 2010.
Nower, J. (1969). "The Traditions of Negro Literature in the United States." *Negro American Literature Forum*, *3*(1). Retrieved from http://www.jstor.org/stable/3041360.
Plotz, D. (2001, October 12). "Higher Education, Lower Ratings." *Slate Magazine*, Retrieved from http://fray.slate.com/id/117119/.
"Popular Romance in the New Millennium Abstracts and Biographies." (n.d.). *McDaniel College*. Retrieved from http://www.mcdaniel.edu/romance/abstracts.htm. Retrieved on August 8, 2011.

The Root. (n.d.). "The Root Rewrites the Western Canon Forget about Paradise Lost and The Canterbury Tales. Here's a list of books that students should be reading in school." *The Root*. Retrieved from http://www.theroot.com/multimedia/root-rewrites-western-canon. Retrieved on March 20, 2011.

Skillz, M. (2010, February 4). "The Next Hustle." *Hip Hop 101A*, Retrieved from http://hiphop101a.blogspot.com/2010/02/next-hustle.html.

Susman, G. (2004, May 19). "Goodnight, Seattle." *Entertainment Weekly*. Retrieved from http://www.ew.com/ew/article/0,,639630,00.html.

Trice, D.T. (March 5, 2009). "New Faces Among Black Studies Scholars." *Los Angeles Times*. Retrieved from http://www.latimes.com/news/nationworld/nation/la-na-black-studies5-2009mar05,0,2952776.story. Retrieved on March 5, 2009.

Tsuruta, D. (n.d.). "Welcome to the Department of Africana Studies: San Francisco State University." *Africana Studies Department History*. Retrieved from http://userwww.sfsu.edu/~afrs/history.html. Retrieved on November 20, 2011.

"Who Will Nikki Tie the Knot with in the Final Episode of 'The Parkers'?" *Jet*. Retrieved from http://findarticles.com/p/articles/mi_m1355/is_19_105/ai_n6181237/. Retrieved on December 1, 2009.

Notes

Chapter 1: Introduction

1. Freire, P. (1970). *Pedagogy of the Oppressed*. New York: Herder and Herder
2. Bernard, R. (2009). *Black and Brown Waves: The Cultural Politics of Young Women of Color and Feminism*. Rotterdam: Sense Publishers.

Chapter 2: Lena James and Felicity Porter

1. Susman, G. (2004, May 19). "Goodnight, Seattle." *Entertainment Weekly*. Retrieved from http://www.ew.com/ew/article/0,,639630,00.html. [Retrieved October, 22, 2009.]
2. Who Will Nikki Tie the Knot with in the Final Episode Of 'THE PARKERS'? (cover story). (2004). *Jet, 105*(19), 54
3. de Moraes, Lisa (September 11, 2008). "Why Did 'Fringe' Unravel? Blame It on the TV God". The Washington Post. http://www.washingtonpost.com/wp-dyn/content/article/2008/09/10/AR2008091003822.html. Retrieved September 22, 2010
4. McGee, S.A., writer, J. Melman, dir., and B. Boulware, executive producer. (1999.) "Grape Nuts." *The Parkers*. United Paramount Network. Television.
5. *A Different World* (TV series). (2009, December 28). Retrieved from http://en.wikipedia.org/w/index.php?title=A_Different_World_(TV_series)&oldid=334565723. Accessed October 22, 2009.
6. Smith, D. (1997, May 1). "Media More Likely to Show Women Talking about Romance Than at a Job, Study Says." *The New York Times*. http://www.nytimes.com/1997/05/01/us/media-

more-likely-to-show-women-talking-about-romance-than-at-a-job-study-says.html?pagewanted=print&src=pm.
7. Gmelch, S. (1998). *Gender on Campus: Issues for College Women*. New Brunswick, N.J.: Rutgers University Press. 320pp.
8. "Federal Work Study: Program Description." (n.d.). Retrieved from http://www2.ed.gov/programs/fws/index.html. Retrieved October 22, 2009.
9. "A Felicity Page. Characters: Elena Tyler." (1999) Retrieved from http://www.felicitypage.com/elena.html. Retrieved October 22, 2009.
10. Fales, S., writer, D. Allen, dir., and M. Carsey, executive producer. (1991). "We've Only Just Begun." *A Different World*. National Broadcasting Company. Television.
11. Miller, G.H., writer, D. Allen, dir., and M. Carsey, executive producer. (1991). "The Dwayne Mutiny." *A Different World*. National Broadcasting Company. Television.
12. ibid.
13. Moseley, R., writer, K. Hardison, dir., and M. Carsey, executive producer. (1993). "Homie, Don't Ya Know Me?" *A Different World*. National Broadcasting Company. Television.
14. ibid.
15. University of Chicago Committee on Educational Television. (1953). "Television and the University." *The School Review*, 61(4). 202–25.
16. Plotz, D. (2001, October 12). "Higher Education, Lower Ratings." *Slate Magazine*. Retrieved from http://fray.slate.com/id/117119/.
17. "A Different World (TV series)." (2009, December 28). *Wikipedia, The Free Encyclopedia*. Retrieved from http://en.wikipedia.org/w/index.php?title=A_Different_World_(TV_series)&oldid=334565723. Retrieved October 22, 2009.
18. Adalian, J. (2009, November 09). "The CW Gives 'Life Unexpected' a 'Gossip Girl' Boost." *The Wrap: Covering Hollywood*. Retrieved from http://www.thewrap.com/ind-column/cw-gives-life-unexpected-gossip-girl-boost-9877.
19. Signorelli, N. (1997). Reflections of the girls in the media. *Fourth Annual Children & Media Conference*, 2–15.
20. Morrissey, T.E. (2009, June 2). "20 Feminist TV Characters." *Jezebel*. Retrieved from http://jezebel.com/5274600/20-feminist-tv-characters.
21. Gibbons, S. (2008). "Media Report to Women: Industry Statistics." Retrieved from http://www.mediareporttowomen.com/statistics.htm.
22. ibid.
23. Rich, A. (1979). *On Lies, Secrets, and Silence: Selected Prose 1966–1978*. New York: Norton.
24. *Center for Screen-Time Qwareness: History*. (2008). Retrieved from http://www.screentime.org/index.php?option=com_content&task=view&id=1&Itemid=2.
25. Arnzen, M. (2005, April 24). *Media Fasting*. Retrieved from http://blogs.setonhill.edu/Mike Arnzen/009181.html.
26. ibid.

Chapter 3: Making Black Studies Political

1. Hare, N. (May 1972). "The Battle of Black Studies." *Black Scholar, 3*, 27–32.

2. To meet the goals of this chapter specifically and many other chapters for this book, it is important to mention that "analysis group" refers to a collective of students (100 total) who participated either by taking my courses in Black Studies over the course of one year (2010–2011), or have been part of the lunch-time lecture series (from 2003–2007) that I created for them. Over time, students were asked to either: fill out surveys, attend open-discussion forums, or sit in on various Black Studies classes. I spent nine years journaling, observing, and chronicling the analysis and events mentioned in this chapter and elsewhere.
3. At the time I began working on this book, many of the students had concerns about tuition increases (with and without aid). Before four years had passed, four students had dropped out completely due to lack of financial support and before the completion of this book, only one of the four returned with financial support (through employment) and completed his degree. The remaining three suggested that they just could not make it.
4. BBC News. (10 November 2010). Archived from the original on 11 November 2011. Retrieved from http://www.bbc.co.uk/news/education-11726822. Retrieved 10 November 2010.
5. Students who received aid were less aware of the tuition-based fees as they were not primarily responsible for payment of such fees.
6. The year before my arrival at this college, there were 2,118 Black students. In 2003, there were 1,891 Black students enrolled at this particular school. (CUNY Factbook, 2003.) The very next year there were only 1,745 Black undergraduates enrolled. In 2010, Black undergraduates made up 11.2 percent of the student body, and in early 2011, that dropped to 11.0 percent.
7. Bernard-Carreño, R. (2010). *Nuyorganics*. New York: Peter Lang.
8. Brown , C. (2006, November 11). What black studies lacks/Phenomenon is either a nod to our common heritage or a rip-off. San Francisco Chronicle, Retrieved from http://www.sfgate.com/opinion/article/What-black-studies-lacks-Phenomenon-is-either-a-2467290.php
9. *The Chicago Tribune*. (2009, March 4). "Can Whites Teach Black Studies?" Retrieved from http://newsblogs.chicagotribune.com/race/2009/03/can-whites-teach-black-studies-.html. Accessed 1/24/2009
10. Allen, R. (1974). "Politics of the Attack on Black Studies" Vol. 6, No. 1, *Black Education: The Future of Black Studies* (September 1974), pp. 2–7.
11. New York Task Force on the Black Male Initiative. (2004). "Final Report of The City University of New York Task Force on the Black Male Initiative." Retrieved from http://www.cuny.edu/academics/initiatives/bmi/task-force-report/TaskForceReport.pdf.
12. City University of New York. (n.d.). "Black Male Initiative: History and Purpose." Retrieved from http://www.cuny.edu/academics/initiatives/bmi/history.html.
13. Norment, N. (2007). *The African American Studies Reader*. Durham, NC: Carolina Academic Press. p. xxix.
14. *Welcome to the Department of Africana Studies!*. (2010, July 28). Retrieved from http://userwww.sfsu.edu/afrs/SFSU Africana Studies website. http://userwww.sfsu.edu/afrs/
15. This was taken from a collection of Black Studies Models and Curricula, from various universities and colleges in the United States. Smith, W. D. (1971). "Black Studies: A Survey of Models and Curricula." *Journal of Black Studies*, *1*(3), 259-272.
16. ibid. xxxv.
17. http://userwww.sfsu.edu/afrs/history.html *African Studies Department History*. (n.d.). Retrieved from http://userwww.sfsu.edu/afrs/history.html Accessed 2/1/2012

18. Cruse, H. (1971). "Black Studies, Interpretation, Methodology and the Relationship to Social Movements." *Afro-American Studies: An Interdisciplinary Journal*, vol. 2. 15.
19. Kilson, M. (1973, March). "Reflections on the Structure and Content of Black Studies." *Journal of Black Studies*, vol. 3, no 3. 297–314.
20. Many of the students were in fact politically active on their campuses and in their communities and through this particular workshop, recruited one another for future events and mobilizations.

Chapter 4: The Black Outcast in the Classroom

1. Lewis, O. (1966). *La Vida: A Puerto Rican Family in the Culture of Poverty—San Juan and New York*. New York: Random House.
2. ibid.
3. Crane, S. (2005). *Maggie: A Girl of the Streets and Other Writings about New York*. New York: Barnes & Noble Classics.
4. Nower, J. (1969). "The Traditions of Negro Literature in the United States." *Negro American Literature Forum*, 3(1). Retrieved from http://www.jstor.org/stable/3041360.
5. Williamson, C., and T. Cluse-Tolar. (2002). "Pimp-controlled Prostitution: Still an Integral Part of Street Life." *Violence Against Women*, 8(9). 1074–1092.
6. Skillz, M. (2010, February 4). "The Next Hustle." Hip Hop 101A. Retrieved from http://hiphop101a.blogspot.com/2010/02/next-hustle.html.
7. Bernard-Carreño, R. (2010). Nuyorganics. New York: Lang.
8. McCord, M. (2009, November 13). The next hustle ex-pimp Robert Beck transformed into writer Iceberg Slim, introducing a new genre for literature, film, and music. Wax poetics, (38), Retrieved from http://www.waxpoetics.com/wax-poetics-magazine/wax-poetics-issue-38
9. ibid.
10. ibid.
11. Beck, R. (1971). *The Naked Soul of Iceberg Slim*. Los Angeles: Holloway House.
12. Goines, D. (1971). *Dopefiend*. Los Angeles: Holloway House.
13. Goines, D. (1972). *Whoreson*. Los Angeles: Holloway House.
14. Goines, D. (1973). *White Man's Justice, Black Man's Grief*. Los Angeles: Holloway House.
15. Allen, E.B. (2004). *Low Road: The Life and Legacy of Donald Goines*. New York: St. Martin's Press.
16. ibid.
17. Williamson, C., & Cluse-Tolar, T. (2002). "Pimp Controlled Prostitution: Still an Integral Part of Street Life." *Violence Against Women*, 8(9), 1074–1092. Retrieved from http://searchfortruth.info/sites/default/files/_pimp-controlled-prostitution_0.pdf
18. Freire, P. (2000). *Pedagogy of the Oppressed*, 30th Anniversary Edition. New York: Continuum.
19. Horton-Stallings, LaMonda. (2003). "'I'm Goin Pimp Whores!': The Goines Factor and the Theory of a Hip-Hop Neo-Slave Narrative." *CR: The New Centennial Review*, vol. 3, no. 3. 175–203.
20. Quinn, E. (2001). *Media, Culture, and the Modern African American Freedom Struggle*. Gainesville, FL: University Press of Florida.
21. ibid.
22. ibid.

23. ibid
24. Morris, V. J. (2007) "Inner City Teens DO Read." http://www.pages.drexel.edu/~gdc27/final/documents/innercityteensdoread.pdf Accessed January 22, 2011
25. Chelton, M.K. (2005). "Perspectives on YA practice: Common YA models of service in public libraries: Advantages and disadvantages." *Young Adult Library Services: The Journal of the Young Adult Library Services Association*, 3(4), 4–11.
26. Fisher, M. (2009). *Black Literate Lives: Historical and Contemporary Perspectives.* New York, NY: Routledge.
27. McCord, M. (2010, February 04). [Web log message]. Retrieved from http://hiphop101a.blogspot.com/2010/02/next-hustle.html
28. Quinn, E. (2001). *Media, Culture, and the Modern African American Freedom Struggle.* Gainesville, FL: University Press of Florida.
29. For example, Magic Don Juan etc.
30. Dickerson, D. (2004). *The End of Blackness: Returning the Souls of Black Folk to Their Rightful Owners.* New York: Pantheon. P. 10.
31. Anderson, E. (1999). *Code of the Street: Decency, Violence, and the Moral Life of the Inner City.* New York: Norton.
32. Note: These courses were not all directly taught out of Black Studies departments, and many of the syllabi were available for review online.
33. Campbell, E. (N.d.). "20th Century Prison Literature." *Mount St Mary's Syllabus.* Retrieved from http://www.msmc.la.edu/PDFFiles/WCsyllabiarchive/Fall2003/eng192fa03.1u.pdf. Retrieved July 8, 2011.
34. "More Romance in the new Millennium." Musings on Romance Fiction from an Academic Perspective. Retrieved from http://teachmetonight.blogspot.com/2011/11/more-romance-in-new-millennium.html. Retrieved on August 8, 2011.
35. One can assume high school and/or college is the target of the population of the article.
36. Farmer, E. (2009). The root rewrites the western canon. TheRoot.Com, Retrieved from http://www.theroot.com/multimedia/root-rewrites-western-canon Accessed January 17, 2012.
37. Souljah, S. (2000). *The Coldest Winter Ever: A Novel.* New York: Pocket.
38. Kincheloe, J. L. (2001). *Getting Beyond the Facts : Teaching Social Studies/Social Sciences in the Twenty-first Century.* (2nd ed., p. 641). New York: Peter Lang
39. It is important to note that many of the shows listed for potential analysis cost $10–$20 per ticket.
40. While I refer to this group as Latino/a here and throughout, this professor refers to them as "Hispanic Americans" in his syllabus.
41. Naison, M., & Graff, K. (2009). Us 5050 hip hop street literature narratives syllabus. Retrieved from http://www.fordham.edu/images/academics/history_department/graduate_syllabus/f09_5050_naison.pdf

Chapter 5: Black Studies Projects

1. Marable, M. (2005). "Intro to African American Studies Syllabus." *Columbia University.* Retrieved from http://www.columbia.edu/cu/ccbh/pdfs/afamsyllabus2005.pdf. Retrieved 15 November 2010.

2. These students were pursuing graduate degrees in Early Childhood Education, Education Studies, and Urban Education.
3. There are anywhere from 3–7 books assigned per class, per semester.
4. It is important to note here that many students under the communal-class model have voted to use their collection of funds to donate to a non-profit organization or gather for a final dinner. Traveling to other states, although inspiring and something we consider every semester, was well over the total monies we were able to collect and produced scheduling conflicts with commuter students.
5. The structural requirements were similar to the structural requirement for the Black Studies Program assignment above, and change according to semester and student population.
6. These results are not limited to just Black Studies students, as I have piloted this program among graduate students in Latino Studies (graduate and undergraduate courses), Women's Studies, Urban Studies, Urban Education and Early Childhood training/academic courses as well.

Chapter 6: Scholarship and Community

1. Important to note here is that the Black Studies program chronicled for this research only offers a minor in the area of study, and this minor only requires 3 courses (2 of which can be electives in the field without any sequence).
2. Retrieved from http://cooperproject.org. Accessed June 2012
3. Harris-Perry, M. (2012). "Black Women's Political Activism Syllabus." Anna Julia Cooper Project Mission. Newcomb College Institute of Tulane University, Fall 2012. Retrieved from http://cooperproject.org/wp-content/uploads/2012/07/BlackWomActivism-Syllabus.pdf. Retrieved 30 July 2012.
4. It is important to note that the school did not offer financial aid for summer courses, thus students were not inclined to take courses on an elective basis for simple interest as opposed to taking summer courses to fulfill requirements.

Rochelle Brock &
Richard Greggory Johnson III,
Executive Editors

Black Studies and Critical Thinking is an interdisciplinary series which examines the intellectual traditions of and cultural contributions made by people of African descent throughout the world. Whether it is in literature, art, music, science, or academics, these contributions are vast and far-reaching. As we work to stretch the boundaries of knowledge and understanding of issues critical to the Black experience, this series offers a unique opportunity to study the social, economic, and political forces that have shaped the historic experience of Black America, and that continue to determine our future. Black Studies and Critical Thinking is positioned at the forefront of research on the Black experience, and is the source for dynamic, innovative, and creative exploration of the most vital issues facing African Americans. The series invites contributions from all disciplines but is specially suited for cultural studies, anthropology, history, sociology, literature, art, and music.

Subjects of interest include (but are not limited to):

- Education
- Sociology
- History
- Media/Communication
- Religion/Theology
- Women's Studies
- Policy Studies
- Advertising
- African American Studies
- Political Science
- LGBT Studies

For additional information about this series or for the submission of manuscripts, please contact Dr. Brock (Indiana University Northwest) at brock2@iun.edu or Dr. Johnson (University of San Francisco) at rgjohnsoniii@usfca.edu.

To order other books in this series, please contact our Customer Service Department:

(800) 770-LANG (within the U.S.)
(212) 647-7706 (outside the U.S.)
(212) 647-7707 FAX

Or browse online by series at www.peterlang.com.

www.ingramcontent.com/pod-product-compliance
Ingram Content Group UK Ltd.
Pitfield, Milton Keynes, MK11 3LW, UK
UKHW021903240426
12048UKWH00038B/1371